THE ANTI-INFLAMMATORY COOKBOOK

Chrissy Freer

THE ANTI-INFLAMMATORY COOKBOOK

100 everyday recipes to soothe your immune system and promote good health

murdoch books
Sydney | London

CONTENTS

introduction

Good inflammation...

The type of inflammation we are most familiar with in our own bodies is acute and, surprisingly, it is a positive thing. It is the body's natural response to an infection caused by bacteria or injury. This is the sort of inflammation we can feel (heat and pain) and see (swollen and red), such as a sore throat or sprained ankle. When acute inflammation occurs, the body sends many types of immune cells (white blood cells/leukocytes) to the site to fight the invading bacteria or virus by releasing mediators. This is what is known as the body's 'immune response'.

It is this cell activity that causes the tell-tale signs of inflammation – the inflammatory mediators released by the immune cells cause more blood and protein to come to the site, which results in the redness and swelling; the excess blood also causes expansion, which is what leads to pain. This also has the potential to damage surrounding tissues by attacking healthy cells instead of the invading pathogens. However, when the body is working as it should, the inflammation resolves quickly, the white blood cells die and are cleared, restoring the equilibrium of the tissues and causing little harm.

...and bad inflammation

The second type of inflammation, chronic or 'silent' inflammation, is a lot less obvious and a lot less positive. Unlike acute, when the immune cells respond rapidly and appropriately to the danger, it is believed that in chronic inflammation there is a problem with the resolution phase. The immune cells have no real infection to strike, so instead they start attacking healthy cells and organs. This results in ongoing long-term inflammation. The consequences of the immune system turning against the body (autoimmune disease) can be serious. Arthritis causes pain and swelling in joints; coeliac disease causes inflammation of the lining of the small bowel; and inflammatory bowel disease causes inflammation of the colon. To complicate matters, low-grade inflammation does not always produce obvious pain or symptoms, making it difficult to identify, let alone measure. This type of low-grade, chronic inflammation can occur for years and potentially increase our risk of age-related illnesses, such as adult asthma, some cancers, heart disease, diabetes and Alzheimer's disease.

The inflammatory mediators produced by the immune cells, such as C-reactive protein, can be used as biomarkers of inflammation. Chronic diseases are associated with elevated levels of these biomarkers.

Causes of chronic inflammation

How and why chronic inflammation occurs is still being investigated by medical researchers; however, several risk factors have been identified. Top of the list is obesity (excess adipose tissue), which has been shown to increase the body's immune response. Adipose tissue is now considered to be an active endocrine organ, being at the crossroad of both metabolism and immunity. Adipose tissue disorders, such as obesity, result in the secretion of inflammatory cytokines, which can result in low-grade inflammation of the whole body. This systemic inflammation can then affect other organs such as the liver, pancreas and muscles, causing a cluster of conditions known as 'metabolic syndrome'. These include insulin resistance, the precursor to type 2 diabetes, and other chronic diseases.

Inherited genes, age-related changes in the immune system, or having an unhealthy gut microbiota can also increase a person's risk of chronic inflammation, in addition to lifestyle factors such as long-term stress, smoking, excess alcohol consumption and a poor diet, especially a diet high in saturated fats.

Food to the rescue

Obesity, metabolic syndrome and diabetes are directly linked to diet-related inflammation. Likewise, it is known that diet can also play an important role in the management of autoimmune conditions, by helping to soothe inflammation and reduce symptoms. It therefore makes good sense to use diet as an easy therapeutic tool to minimise the impact of inflammatory conditions.

An anti-inflammatory diet is a way of eating for life rather than a 'diet' and the basic principles are relatively simple. There are foods that create an inflammatory response in the body, such as processed carbohydrates and refined sugars (these can contribute to raised blood sugar levels, which increase the pro-inflammatory chemicals secreted by our immune cells) and saturated fats (which also turn on inflammatory mediators). A diet high in saturated fats, processed carbohydrates and refined sugars is also linked to obesity, of course, making it a lose-lose situation.

On the plus side, there are foods that have an anti-inflammatory effect on the body, such as omega-3 fatty acids, monounsaturated fats, dietary fibre, polyphenols and antioxidants. An anti-inflammatory way of eating simply aims to increase these foods while decreasing the foods that create an inflammatory response.

So, what should we be eating?

Plenty of vegetables and fruit are a pivotal part of the anti-inflammatory diet, and for good reason. Low in both kilojoules and fat, these are a powerful tool for weight management as well as being rich in a host of vitamins and minerals, dietary fibre and disease-fighting phytonutrients. Eat a rainbow of variety, as each colour has something unique to offer. For example, anthocyanin pigments (blueberries, blackberries, cherries, beetroot), polyphenols (grapes), carotenoids (orange and red veg), sulforaphane compounds (cruciferous vegetables) and free radical-fighting antioxidants in dark green leafy vegetables may all potentially boost immunity and reduce inflammation. Aim for at least five serves of veg and two-to-three of fruit per day.

Legumes are nutrition powerhouses, being rich in plant protein, dietary fibre and several nutrients including iron, zinc, magnesium, potassium and B vitamins. Their high fibre content is linked to reducing C-reactive protein, a marker of inflammation. Even better, soy beans are also a valuable source of the omega-3 fatty acid ALA.

Seafood is an excellent source of high-quality protein and is rich in several micronutrients including zinc, iron, iodine, selenium, vitamin A and D. It is, however, the omega-3 (DHA and EPA) content that makes seafood a true anti-inflammatory hero. All species contain omega-3;

however, oily fish such as salmon, sardines, mackerel, anchovies, trout and tuna are particularly good sources. Aim for at least three serves per week to gain the benefits.

Wholegrains comprise all three parts of the grain: the endosperm (starch component), the bran (fibre layer) and the germ (the protein, fat and mineral component). Wholegrains are rich in dietary fibre and may lower levels of C-reactive protein in the blood. In contrast, refined grains have had the bran and germ removed, leaving only the starchy endosperm, so they are not only lacking in nutrients, but are also associated with increased inflammation. Brown rice, quinoa, buckwheat, millet, amaranth and sorghum are all excellent wholegrain choices.

Fresh and dried spices are a wonderful way to add flavour without adding calories, fat, sugar or sodium. Turmeric contains the active compound curcumin, which acts as a powerful antioxidant, blocking inflammatory cytokines. Likewise, ginger, garlic, cinnamon and cayenne pepper all contain active compounds with natural anti-inflammatory properties.

Many nuts, seeds and oils are rich sources of monounsaturated and polyunsaturated fats, and therefore contain omega 6 and omega-3 fatty acids. It is the quantities of each that are important, hence why some nuts and seeds are better for inflammation. Walnuts, linseeds and chia seeds (and their oils) are high in the anti-inflammatory omega-3 fatty acid ALA. Some nuts are rich in the antioxidant vitamin E, also known to have anti-inflammatory properties. Extra virgin olive oil is rich in monounsaturated fatty acids, as well as containing anti-inflammatory and antioxidant compounds. Macadamia and avocado oil are also excellent choices, being predominantly monounsaturated, so relatively low in omega 6.

OMEGA-3 FATTY ACIDS

Omega-3 fats are polyunsaturated essential fatty acids that can reduce inflammation. They can make changes to the fatty acid composition of cell membranes that play an important role in immune cell signalling pathways. Likewise, the hormones responsible for the resolution phase of inflammation, when the white blood cells die and are cleared away, are derived from omega-3 fatty acids.

There are three kinds of omega-3 fatty acids: ALA, which is found in vegetable oils, walnuts, linseeds, chia and soy products; DHA and EPA, which are found in seafood, fish and fish oils.

OMEGA 6 FATTY ACIDS

Omega 6 fats are also polyunsaturated essential fatty acids, found in vegetable oils, nuts, seeds and meat – but it is believed that, conversely, these fats have an inflammatory effect on the body. The theories are very much in debate, with emerging evidence suggesting that rather than avoiding or reducing omega-6, we can simply increase amounts of omega-3 consumed, to improve the ratio.

Although highly nutritious, nuts, seeds and oils are energy dense, so do need to be consumed in moderation.

All meats are excellent sources of complete protein, which means they contains all nine of the essential amino acids our bodies need from food. Depending on the type of meat, it can also be a rich source of iron, zinc, vitamin B6, B12 and niacin. On the flip side, the fat content can vary from 5 to 35 per cent and the fat you can see on meat is saturated, which can have an inflammatory effect. Therefore, it makes sense to choose lean cuts of meat, reduce your intake of red meat, trim off all excess fat before or after cooking, and enjoy meat in moderation.

Reduced-fat dairy products are also an excellent source of protein and are packed with dietary calcium and vitamin D, essential for healthy bones and teeth. Dairy products do contain saturated fat, and this can be high in products such as butter, cheese and cream. For those who can tolerate and enjoy dairy, it is simply about making good choices. Natural yoghurt is lower in fat than other varieties, choose reduced-fat milk and opt for ricotta and cottage cheese, which are naturally lower in fat. Parmesan, although high in fat, is packed with flavour so you only need to use a little.

And what should we avoid?

Processed foods are typically high in fat, especially saturated and trans fats, and high in sodium and added sugars. Processed foods generally contain little nutritive value yet are high in calories, therefore increasing the risk of obesity and inflammation. Likewise, alcohol is high in calories and sugar, with no nutritional benefit. On the flip side, some studies have suggested a moderate red wine intake can reduce some inflammatory markers. It seems prudent to say that if you are going to drink alcohol, less is best.

The role of gluten

For some inflammatory conditions, such as coeliac disease, it is recommended to avoid eating grains that contain gluten. Many people who are following an anti-inflammatory diet also choose to avoid gluten and for this reason, all recipes in this book are gluten free. In the ingredients lists we have reminded you to use gluten-free versions of bread, pasta, flour, stock and Asian sauces; and whilst they typically should not contain gluten, it is always essential to check labels for ingredients such as mustard, chipotle sauce, pickled ginger, wasabi and flavoured vinegars. Likewise, for those who do not need to avoid gluten, we have given you the option to use wholegrain versions of bread, flour and pasta as required, so you can choose what works for your own dietary needs.

Planning your new way of eating

It can sometimes be daunting, as well as exciting and positive, when changing the way you eat and cook, so to kickstart your anti-inflammatory lifestyle we have included two weeks of easy meal plans on pages 234 and 235. These give you simple ideas for breakfast, lunch and dinner, plus snacks, every day for two weeks, to set you on the path towards a healthier, and more delicious, way of eating, every day.

breakfast

vegan (see tip)

This gluten-free muesli runs rings around the commercial varieties. Packed with protein, complex carbohydrates and dietary fibre, plus almonds and seeds for a good dose of anti-inflammatory mono and polyunsaturated fats, this is just what you need to start your day.

Muesli with dried apple, pepitas and almonds

Preparation time: 15 minutes
Cooking time: None
Makes about 500 g (6½ cups)

- 75 g (1½ cups) puffed amaranth
- 22 g (1½ cups) puffed millet
- 80 g (1 cup) rice bran flakes
- 100 g (½ cup) roasted buckwheat
- 50 g (½ cup) dried apple, chopped
- 85 g (½ cup) sweetened dried cranberries
- 100 g (⅔ cup) almonds, coarsely chopped
- 40 g (½ cup) pepitas (pumpkin seeds)
- 2 tablespoons linseeds
- 40 g (¼ cup) sunflower seeds
- reduced-fat milk, to serve (see tips)

Mix all the ingredients in a large bowl and store in an airtight container until needed.

tips For a vegan version, use unsweetened soy, almond or coconut milk.

This muesli will keep for about 2 weeks in an airtight container in a cool dark place.

vegan

This is a baked granola recipe you can feel really good about! Unlike most commercial granolas, it contains no added oil and is sweetened only with natural sugars from the date purée. Full of nuts and seeds, it's rich and filling, so you don't need a large serving.

Nutty buckwheat granola with dates and seeds

Preparation time: 20 minutes
Cooking time: 35 minutes
Makes about 500 g (3 cups)

100 g (3½ oz) medjool dates, pitted and chopped
2 teaspoons natural vanilla extract
1 teaspoon ground cinnamon
195 g (1 cup) buckwheat kernels
40 g (¼ cup) pepitas (pumpkin seeds)
40 g (¼ cup) sunflower seeds
40 g (¼ cup) raw walnut halves, roughly chopped
30 g (¼ cup) unsalted raw cashew nuts, roughly chopped
35 g (½ cup) shredded coconut
20 g (1 cup) puffed millet

1 Soak the dates in 80 ml (⅓ cup) of boiling water for 10 minutes. Transfer the dates and liquid to a food processor, add the vanilla and cinnamon and process to a smooth paste.

2 Preheat the oven to 150°C (300°F). Line a large baking tray with baking paper.

3 Combine the buckwheat, seeds and nuts in a bowl, add the date paste and toss until evenly coated. Spread in a single layer on the tray.

4 Bake for 30 minutes or until golden and crisp, stirring every 10 minutes. Add the coconut and millet and bake for 3–4 minutes or until the coconut is just golden. Cool completely before serving.

tip The granola will keep in an airtight container for up to 4 weeks.

(pictured page 17)

vegan (see tips)

Quinoa works beautifully in this warming porridge. Naturally gluten free, this grain is rich in plant protein and contains all the essential amino acids. The sweetened dried cranberries add a little natural tanginess and the sprinkling of seeds gives a good dose of omega-3 fatty acids.

Quinoa and cranberry porridge with power seed sprinkle

Preparation time: 10 minutes
Cooking time: 15 minutes
Serves 4

200 g (1 cup) quinoa, rinsed

250 ml (1 cup) reduced-fat milk, plus extra to serve (see tips)

40 g (1/4 cup) sweetened dried cranberries

1/2 teaspoon natural vanilla extract

POWER SEED SPRINKLE

40 g (1/4 cup) sunflower seeds

40 g (1/4 cup) pepitas (pumpkin seeds)

1 tablespoon linseeds (flaxseeds)

1 tablespoon sesame seeds

1 teaspoon coconut sugar

1/2 teaspoon ground cinnamon

1 tablespoon chia seeds

1 For the power seed sprinkle, preheat the oven to 180°C (375°F). Line a large baking tray with baking paper. Combine all the ingredients and spread over the tray. Bake for 5 minutes or until lightly toasted. Cool.

2 Meanwhile, combine the quinoa and 500 ml (2 cups) cold water in a large saucepan. Bring to the boil, cover, reduce the heat to low and simmer for 10 minutes. Add the milk, cranberries and vanilla and cook, stirring, for 5 minutes or until the porridge is thick and creamy.

tips Serve the porridge topped with a little power seed sprinkle (you will have some left over for next time) and with milk.

For a vegan version, use unsweetened soy, almond or coconut milk.

The power seed sprinkle will keep in an airtight container for up to 2 weeks.

(pictured page 16)

Quinoa and cranberry porridge with power seed sprinkle

(see recipe page 15)

Nutty buckwheat granola
with dates and seeds

(see recipe page 14)

dairy free (see tip)

I love eggs for breakfast. Packed with protein, they really stay the course and keep me full until lunchtime. A serve of veggies at breakfast not only adds a good amount of dietary fibre, a key nutrient for decreasing inflammation, but is also a great way to increase your overall intake for the day.

Kale eggs with smoked salmon and broccolini

Preparation time: 10 minutes
Cooking time: 5 minutes
Serves 2

180 g (6¼ oz) broccolini, cut into short lengths

4 eggs

2 tablespoons reduced-fat milk (see tip)

1 teaspoon extra virgin olive oil

1 garlic clove, crushed

50 g (1¾ oz) kale, chopped

75 g (2¾ oz) sliced smoked salmon

Lime wedges, to serve

1 Steam the broccolini for 2 minutes, then drain.

2 Whisk the eggs and milk together. Season with sea salt and freshly ground black pepper.

3 Heat the oil in a frying pan over medium heat. Add the broccolini and garlic and cook, stirring, for 1 minute. Add the kale, stir until just wilted and remove from the pan.

4 Reduce the heat to low–medium. Add the egg mixture and stir gently with a wooden spoon, bringing the egg from the edge of the pan to the centre. Continue until almost set. Gently stir in the broccolini mixture and season to taste.

5 Serve hot with smoked salmon and a squeeze of lime juice.

tip For a dairy-free version, use unsweetened soy, almond, or coconut milk.

dairy free • vegetarian

Replace bread with sweet potato 'toast' for a nutrient-rich breakfast. Sweet potatoes are packed with carotenoids – essential for growth, cell development and healthy skin – and which have potential anti-inflammatory properties. If short of time, toast sweet potato slices in your toaster until tender (without the oil and paprika). They may take 2–3 'toasts'.

Sweet potato toast with poached egg, avocado, tomato and herb salad

Preparation time: 5 minutes
Cooking time: 25 minutes
Serves 4

- 750 g (1 lb 10 oz) sweet potato, peeled
- 1 teaspoon paprika
- Extra virgin olive oil spray, for coating
- 1 small avocado, diced
- 200 g (7 oz) grape tomatoes, halved
- ¼ cup fresh mint leaves
- ¼ cup fresh flat-leaf (Italian) parsley leaves
- Pinch dried red chilli flakes
- 2 teaspoons lemon juice
- 2 teaspoons extra virgin olive oil
- 4 eggs, poached, to serve

1 Preheat the oven to 200°C (400°F). Line a baking tray with baking paper. Cut the sweet potato into eight 5 mm (¼ inch) thick slices. Place on the tray, sprinkle with paprika and lightly spray with oil. Bake for 25 minutes, turning halfway through cooking, or until golden and tender.

2 Meanwhile, combine the avocado, tomatoes, mint, parsley, chilli flakes, lemon juice and oil in a small bowl. Season with salt and pepper.

3 To serve, top 2 slices of sweet potato 'toast' with a poached egg. Serve with the avocado salad.

vegan

Berries are rich in polyphenols, with known anti-inflammatory properties. The addition of LSA also provides omega-3 fatty acids and a delicious nutty taste. I like to use coconut water instead of juice to keep the sugar levels down.

Berry smoothie with avocado and coconut water

Preparation time: 5 minutes
Cooking time: None
Serves 2

400 ml (14 fl oz) coconut water

195 g (1½ cups) frozen mixed berries (see tips)

½ avocado, chopped

1 tablespoon LSA (linseed, sunflower seed and almond meal) blend (see tips)

Put all the ingredients in a blender and blend on high speed until smooth. Serve immediately.

tips Frozen berries are often more convenient and they actually work better than fresh here, resulting in a thick, cold smoothie.

LSA blend is available from the health-food section of supermarkets.

vegan

Green smoothies are a great way to add a serve of vegetables to your daily intake. Chia seeds are loaded with anti-inflammatory omega-3 fatty acids, and will help keep you feeling full due to their high fibre content.

Green zing smoothie with mango and chia

Preparation time: 5 minutes
Cooking time: None
Serves 2

400 ml (14 fl oz) coconut water

270 g (1½ cups) seedless green grapes

1 large mango, chopped (see tip)

30 g (⅔ cup) baby English spinach or kale leaves

¼ cup coriander (cilantro) or mint leaves

1 tablespoon chia seeds

Handful of ice cubes

Put all the ingredients in a blender and blend on high speed until smooth and thick. Serve immediately.

tip When mango is out of season, replace it with any other fresh fruit – bananas or kiwi fruit work well.

dairy free • vegetarian

The secret to great banana bread is to use super-ripe bananas – that way you only need to add a little extra sweetness. I like to use honey, but you can replace that with rice malt syrup or maple syrup if you wish.

Banana bread

Preparation time: 15 minutes
Cooking time: 45 minutes
Makes 10 slices

35 g (1/4 cup) coconut flour
1 teaspoon ground ginger
1 teaspoon ground cinnamon
pinch of ground nutmeg
1½ teaspoons gluten-free baking powder
75 g (3/4 cup) almond meal
25 g (1/4 cup) desiccated coconut
4 large ripe bananas
3 eggs
2 tablespoons single origin floral honey
2 tablespoons macadamia oil or melted coconut oil
1 teaspoon vanilla bean extract

1 Preheat the oven to 180°C (350°F). Lightly spray a 10 x 20 cm (4 x 8 inch) non-stick loaf tin with oil. Line the base and long sides with baking paper, extending over the sides.

2 Sift the flour, ginger, cinnamon, nutmeg and baking powder into a large bowl. Stir in the almond meal and coconut. Make a well in the centre.

3 Mash 3 of the bananas in a medium bowl. Add the eggs, honey, oil and vanilla. Pour the banana mixture into the well in the flour mixture. Fold in until just combined.

4 Spoon the mixture into the tin and smooth the surface with the back of a spoon. Cut the remaining banana into 4 long slices and gently press into the surface. Bake for 45 minutes or until a skewer inserted into the centre comes out with a few moist crumbs. Cover the top with foil if browning too quickly (see tips). Set aside in the tin for 5 minutes, then turn out onto a wire rack to cool.

tips This loaf can be stored in an airtight container for up to 3 days, or frozen for up to 1 month. Wrap individual slices in plastic wrap to freeze.

The high nut content of this bread causes it to brown quickly. Check after 20–30 minutes of cooking time and cover the top with foil if necessary.

vegan

These chia pots are ideal to make the night before, then simply top with yoghurt and berries when ready to serve. Chia seeds may be tiny but they pack a big nutritional punch, with the highest plant-based content of omega-3 fatty acids.

Choc chia, coconut and blueberry pots

Preparation time: 10 minutes (plus 4 hours chilling time)
Cooking time: None
Makes 4

625 ml (2½ cups) unsweetened coconut or almond milk

1½ tablespoons cacao powder

4 fresh dates, pitted, chopped

½ teaspoon ground cinnamon

1 teaspoon vanilla bean paste

80 g (½ cup) white chia seeds

160 g (⅔ cup) coconut yoghurt

125 g (¾ cup) fresh or thawed frozen blueberries

Pure maple syrup, to drizzle (optional)

1 Blend the coconut milk, cacao, dates, cinnamon and vanilla in a blender on high speed until smooth. Transfer to a large bowl.

2 Add the chia seeds and stir to combine. Cover and place in the fridge to chill for 4 hours or overnight, until thick (see tip).

3 To serve, spoon the chia mixture into 4 serving glasses. Top each with some coconut yoghurt and blueberries. Drizzle with a little maple syrup, if using.

tip These pots will keep, covered, in the fridge for up to 3 days.

Butter bean, chilli and corn fritters with cucumber salad

(see recipe page 26)

Baked eggs and beans with hummus toasts

(see recipe page 27)

vegetarian

Butter beans are a nutritious addition to veggie fritters: they're extremely low in fat, high in protein and rich in dietary fibre. They also add body and texture, which means you need only a little flour to bind the mixture.

Butter bean, chilli and corn fritters with cucumber salad

Preparation time: 20 minutes
Cooking time: 30 minutes
Serves 4

1 tablespoon extra virgin olive oil

400 g (2 cups) fresh corn kernels (see tips)

½ red capsicum (pepper), diced

4 spring onions (scallions), thinly sliced

1 long green chilli, seeded and finely chopped

2 garlic cloves, crushed

400 g (14 oz) can butter beans, rained and rinsed (see tips)

2 eggs

75 g (½ cup) gluten free or wholemeal plain (all-purpose) flour

2 tablespoons chopped flat-leaf (Italian) parsley

Salad leaves, to serve (optional)

CUCUMBER SALAD

2 Lebanese (short) cucumbers

2 tablespoons natural yoghurt

1 tablespoon chopped flat-leaf (Italian) parsley

1 tablespoon chopped dill

1 tablespoon lemon juice

1 Heat 1 teaspoon of the oil in a large non-stick frying pan over medium heat and cook the corn, capsicum, spring onions and chilli, stirring, for 2 minutes or until just tender. Add the garlic and stir for 30 seconds. Transfer to a large bowl and leave to cool.

2 Process the butter beans and eggs in a food processor until smooth. Add the flour and process until well combined. Add to the corn mixture, then stir in the parsley. Season with sea salt and black pepper.

3 Heat the remaining oil in a large non-stick frying pan over medium–high heat. Add ¼ cup of mixture per fritter, cooking three at a time. Cook for 3 minutes each side or until golden and cooked through. Keep warm while you cook the rest, using a little more oil if necessary.

4 To make the cucumber salad, peel the cucumber into ribbons, stopping when you reach the seeds. Stir together the cucumber ribbons, yoghurt, parsley, dill and lemon juice.

5 Serve the hot fritters with the cucumber salad and salad leaves, if using.

tips You'll need 2–3 cobs of corn for this recipe.

You can replace the butter beans with cannellini beans.

(pictured page 24)

vegetarian

Eggs and beans provide a winning combo of protein and dietary fibre, guaranteed to keep you feeling full and satisfied. You'll need a large non-stick frying pan with a lid for this recipe.

Baked eggs and beans with hummus toasts

Preparation time: 20 minutes
Cooking time: 20 minutes
Serves 4

2 teaspoons extra virgin olive oil

1 red onion, finely chopped

2 garlic cloves, crushed

1 long red chilli, seeded and finely chopped

1 teaspoon paprika

1 teaspoon ground cumin

½ teaspoon dried oregano

400 g (14 oz) can cherry tomatoes or diced tomatoes

255 g (1½ cups) cooked red kidney beans (see tip)

4 eggs

30 g (1 oz) reduced-fat feta cheese, crumbled (optional)

4 slices gluten-free or wholegrain bread

2 tablespoons hummus

Chopped flat-leaf (Italian) parsley, to garnish

1 Heat the olive oil in a large non-stick frying pan over medium heat. Add the onion and cook, stirring, for 5 minutes or until softened. Add the garlic, chilli, paprika, cumin and oregano and cook, stirring, for 1 minute or until fragrant.

2 Stir in the tomatoes and 80 ml (⅓ cup) water. Add the beans and simmer for 10 minutes or until the sauce has thickened.

3 Make four holes in the sauce with a wooden spoon. Carefully crack an egg into each hole, then crumble the feta over the top, if using. Cover the pan and simmer until the eggs are cooked to your liking (about 4 minutes for soft-poached).

4 Meanwhile, toast the bread and spread it with the hummus. Garnish the eggs with chopped parsley and serve with the hummus toasts.

tip You can replace the cooked kidney beans with 400 g (14 oz) canned beans, rinsed. Look for a brand with little or no added salt.

(pictured page 25)

dairy free • vegan (see tips)

Make this jam when strawberries are in season – when they're abundant and inexpensive. Chia seeds thicken the jam plus add a good dose of omega-3 fatty acids and dietary fibre, while honey replaces the usual sugar as a sweetener.

Strawberry, chia and ginger jam

Preparation time: 10 minutes
Cooking time: 35 minutes
Makes 500 ml (2 cups)

750 g (about 5 cups) fresh or frozen strawberries, hulled and sliced (see tips)

175 g (1/2 cup) single origin floral honey

11/2 tablespoons lemon juice

2 teaspoons finely grated ginger

1 teaspoon natural vanilla extract

1 tablespoon chia seeds

1 Combine the strawberries, honey, lemon juice, ginger and vanilla in a saucepan over medium heat. Bring to a simmer and cook, stirring occasionally, for 30–35 minutes or until reduced and thickened (see tips). Remove from the heat and stir in the chia seeds.

2 Transfer immediately to a sterilised jar (see tips). Cover, cool and refrigerate. The jam will keep for several weeks.

tips You can use any combination of berries you like – raspberries, blueberries and blackberries all work well.

The jam will continue to thicken off the heat after the chia seeds are added.

To sterilise the jar, simply put it through the hot cycle in a dishwasher. Alternatively, wash and rinse it thoroughly, then heat in the oven at 160°C (320°F) for 20 minutes.

For a vegan version, replace the honey with rice malt syrup.

snacks & starters

dairy free

Cannellini beans are high in protein and fibre, contain various antioxidant and anti-inflammatory compounds, have a low GI and are virtually fat free. Their delicious creamy texture works perfectly in this dip.

Cannellini bean, tuna and caper dip

Preparation time: 10 minutes
Cooking time: None
Serves 6–8

400 g (14 oz) can cannellini beans, drained and rinsed

185 g (6½ oz) can tuna in olive oil, drained, oil reserved

1 tablespoon lemon juice

1 tablespoon salted baby capers, rinsed and chopped

2 tablespoons chopped flat-leaf (Italian) parsley, plus extra to garnish

½ small red onion, very finely chopped

Extra virgin olive oil, to garnish (optional)

Vegetables, such as snow peas (mangetout), carrots, radishes and asparagus, for dipping

1 Process the cannellini beans, tuna, 1 tablespoon of the reserved oil and the lemon juice in a food processor until almost smooth, adding a little extra oil if necessary.

2 Add the capers, parsley and most of the onion and pulse until combined, leaving some texture. Season to taste with black pepper.

3 Garnish with the remaining onion, extra parsley and a drizzle of olive oil, if using. Serve with vegetables for dipping.

tip This dip will keep in an airtight container in the fridge for 3 days.

vegan

Roasted sweet potato adds sweetness to this version of hummus, and cashews add a delicious creaminess. Try serving it on crisp breads, as a healthy alternative to mayonnaise in sandwiches, or with vegetable sticks for a nutritious snack.

Roasted sweet potato and cashew hummus

Preparation time: 15 minutes
Cooking time: 25 minutes
Makes 2 cups

- **300 g (10½ oz) sweet potato, peeled and coarsely chopped**
- **Extra virgin olive oil spray**
- **400 g (14 oz) can chickpeas, drained and rinsed (see tips)**
- **2 tablespoons roasted unsalted cashews, coarsely chopped**
- **1 tablespoon tahini**
- **1 garlic clove, crushed**
- **½ teaspoon ground cumin**
- **½ teaspoon sweet paprika, plus extra to garnish**
- **Pinch of dried chilli flakes (optional)**
- **60 ml (¼ cup) extra virgin olive oil, plus extra to garnish**
- **1 tablespoon lemon juice**

1 Preheat the oven to 200°C (400°F). Line a small baking tray with baking paper. Place the sweet potato on the prepared tray and spray lightly with olive oil to coat. Bake for 25 minutes or until golden and tender. Set aside to cool.

2 Process the chickpeas, cashews, tahini, garlic, spices and sweet potato in a food processor until well combined. Add the olive oil, lemon juice and 2–3 tablespoons warm water. Process until smooth and creamy. Season to taste with sea salt and freshly ground black pepper. Serve drizzled with extra olive oil and sprinkled with extra paprika.

tips You can replace the canned chickpeas with 225 g (1⅓ cups) cooked chickpeas. When you're cooking dried chickpeas for this or any other hummus recipe, process the cooked chickpeas while they're still hot. This way, the skins will disintegrate and the hummus will be smooth.

Hummus will keep in an airtight container in the refrigerator for up to 4 days.

(pictured page 36)

dairy free • vegan (see tips)

Roasted chickpeas make a delicious and super-healthy snack on the go. They have a low GI and are naturally gluten- and dairy-free. They make a great low-fat substitute for roasted nuts and they're lunchbox-friendly too.

Honey spice roasted chickpeas

Preparation time: 5 minutes (plus 20 minutes draining)
Cooking time: 30 minutes
Serves 2

400 g (14 oz) can chickpeas, drained and rinsed (see tips)

1 tablespoon single origin pure floral honey

1 teaspoon ground cinnamon

Pinch of freshly grated nutmeg

Extra virgin olive oil spray

1 Preheat the oven to 200°C (400°F). Line a baking tray with baking paper. Put the chickpeas on a plate lined with paper towel and set aside for 20 minutes to remove excess moisture.

2 Combine the chickpeas, honey, cinnamon and nutmeg in a bowl. Stir to coat the chickpeas in the honey. Place on the prepared tray and spray lightly with olive oil to coat.

3 Roast for 30 minutes, gently shaking the tray every 10 minutes. The chickpeas should be dark golden and slightly crisp. Remove from the oven and set aside to cool. The chickpeas will continue to become crisp as they cool.

tips You can replace the canned chickpeas with 225 g (1⅓ cups) cooked chickpeas.

It's essential to remove as much moisture from the chickpeas as possible so that they become crisp when cooked. They will keep in an airtight container for 2 days.

For a vegan version, replace the honey with rice malt syrup.

(pictured page 37)

Roasted sweet potato and cashew hummus

(see recipe page 34)

Honey spice roasted chickpeas

(see recipe page 35)

vegetarian (see tips)

Flour made from the whole sorghum grain has a neutral, slightly sweet flavour that lends itself perfectly to baking. Highly nutritious, it has a lower GI than many flours, is a good source of fibre and is naturally gluten free.

Roasted garlic, parmesan and olive flatbread

Preparation time: 15 minutes (plus 30 minutes proving)
Cooking time: 1 hour 10 minutes
Serves 10–12

2 garlic bulbs
2 tablespoons extra virgin olive oil, plus extra for drizzling
3 teaspoons single origin floral honey
7 g (2 teaspoons) dried yeast
225 g (1½ cups) sorghum flour
70 g (½ cup) millet flour
½ teaspoon xanthan gum
50 g (½ cup) almond meal
35 g (⅓ cup) finely grated parmesan cheese (see tips)
2 eggs, lightly beaten
10 large green olives, pitted
Rosemary sprigs, to garnish

1 Preheat the oven to 180°C (350°F). Slice the top from each garlic bulb, leaving the cloves attached at the base, and remove the excess papery skin, leaving at least one layer. Place each bulb on a piece of foil, drizzle with a little oil and wrap to enclose. Bake for 45 minutes or until the garlic is very tender and light golden. Cool completely and then squeeze the garlic pulp from the skins.

2 Whisk the honey and yeast with 125 ml (½ cup) water and leave in a warm place for 10 minutes or until frothy. Meanwhile, line a baking tray with baking paper.

3 Sift the flours and xanthan gum into a bowl. Stir in the almond meal, parmesan, roasted garlic pulp and a pinch of sea salt. Make a well in the centre, add the egg, oil and the yeast mixture and stir with a wooden spoon to form a soft dough. Turn out onto a work surface and knead for 30 seconds or until smooth. Press the dough into a 30 cm (12 inch) round on the tray. Cover with a damp tea towel and leave in a warm place for 30 minutes or until slightly risen.

4 Press dimples into the dough with your fingers, then press the olives into the dough. Decorate with rosemary and drizzle with a little extra oil. Bake for 20–25 minutes or until golden brown and crisp. Cool for 5 minutes, then transfer to a wire rack. Serve warm.

tips For a vegetarian version, use parmesan made with non-animal rennet.

The bread is best served as soon as it's made, but it can be reheated.

dairy free

This dish makes a great starter and is good for you, too. Ocean trout, like all oily fish, is rich in essential omega-3 fatty acids. The salad of earthy raw beetroot cuts the richness of the trout. The fish takes 24 hours to cure, so leave yourself enough time.

Citrus-cured ocean trout gravlax with raw beetroot salad

Preparation time: 30 minutes (plus 24 hours curing)
Cooking time: None
Serves 6

2 x 200 g (7 oz) ocean trout fillets, skin on

2 beetroot (beets), cut into matchsticks

4 small radishes, cut into matchsticks

1 tablespoon chopped dill

2 teaspoons extra virgin olive oil

2 teaspoons lemon juice

1 tablespoon sunflower seeds, lightly toasted

CITRUS CURE

160 g (½ cup) coarse sea salt

2 tablespoons rice malt syrup

2 tablespoons chopped dill

30 ml (1 fl oz) gin

2 teaspoons finely grated lemon zest

2 teaspoons finely grated lime zest

1 teaspoon crushed black peppercorns

1 Mix together all the ingredients for the citrus cure.

2 Spread a third of the cure in a large non-metallic dish. Add the trout fillets, skin side down, in a single layer. Spread the rest of the cure over the trout. Cover and refrigerate for 24 hours, turning after 12 hours.

3 Scrape the cure from the trout, rinse briefly and pat dry with paper towel. Thinly slice the trout on a slight angle, cutting towards the skin (discard the skin).

4 Mix together the beetroot, radish and dill. Whisk the olive oil and lemon juice in a separate bowl.

5 To serve, arrange the trout slices, overlapping slightly, on serving plates. Top with the raw beetroot salad, drizzle with the dressing and sprinkle with the toasted sunflower seeds.

tip The cured trout will keep, wrapped in plastic, in an airtight container in the fridge for up to 1 week.

vegan

Edamame make a delicious and healthy high-protein and high-fibre snack, as well as providing a good dose of plant-based omega-3 fatty acids. They need to be removed from their outer pods before eating, so serve them with a bowl for the discarded pods.

Edamame with chilli salt

Preparation time: 5 minutes
Cooking time: 5 minutes
Serves 4

½ teaspoon dried chilli flakes

½ teaspoon sea salt

250 g (9 oz) fresh or frozen edamame (soy beans) (see tip)

1 tablespoon gluten-free salt-reduced soy sauce

½ teaspoon sesame oil

1 Combine the chilli flakes and salt in a small bowl and set aside.

2 Cook the edamame in a saucepan of boiling water for 2 minutes or until just tender. Drain.

3 Transfer the edamame to a serving bowl. Drizzle with the soy sauce and sesame oil. Sprinkle with the chilli salt. Serve immediately.

tip Fresh soy beans (edamame) can be tricky to find. Frozen soy beans are available all year round, and can be found in the frozen vegetable section of supermarkets and Asian food stores.

vegetarian (see tip)

Kale chips are completely addictive and, luckily, they make the perfect guilt-free snack. Make sure you spread the kale in a single layer on the baking trays so the leaves become deliciously crisp. They are best eaten the day they are made.

Kale chips, three ways

Preparation time: 5 minutes
Cooking time: 10–12 minutes
Serves 4

1 teaspoon ground cumin

1 teaspoon ground coriander

¼ teaspoon ground cinnamon

1 teaspoon pure maple syrup

2 teaspoons extra virgin olive oil

1 large bunch curly green kale, trimmed, torn into bite-size pieces

1 Preheat the oven to 180°C (350°F). Line 2 large baking trays with baking paper.

2 Combine the cumin, coriander, cinnamon, maple syrup and oil in a large bowl. Add the kale and toss until evenly coated. Spread the kale out in a single layer on the prepared trays.

3 Bake for 10–12 minutes, swapping the trays halfway through cooking, or until the leaves are crisp. Set aside to completely cool. Place in an airtight container.

Smoked paprika and lemon

In step 2, combine 1 teaspoon smoked paprika, 2 teaspoons finely grated lemon zest and 2 teaspoons extra virgin olive oil in a large bowl. Add the kale and toss until evenly coated. Spread the kale out in a single layer on the trays and bake as before.

Parmesan chilli

In step 2, combine ½ teaspoon dried chilli flakes and 2 teaspoons extra virgin olive oil in a large bowl. Add the kale and toss until evenly coated. Spread the kale out in a single layer on the trays and sprinkle with 2 tablespoons finely grated parmesan. Bake as before.

tip For a vegetarian version, use parmesan made with non-animal rennet.

dairy free

Wholegrain brown rice takes longer to break down in your body than white rice, so this sushi will help your blood sugar levels remain stable throughout the day.

Sushi with spicy sesame chicken and avocado

Preparation time: 30 minutes (plus 1 hour marinating and 30 minutes chilling)
Cooking time: 45 minutes
Makes 4 large rolls

300 g (1½ cups) medium-grain or short-grain brown rice

60 ml (¼ cup) seasoned rice vinegar (see tip)

60 ml (¼ cup) white vinegar

4 sheets nori

1 Lebanese (short) cucumber, cut into 5 cm (2 inch) batons

½ avocado, peeled, stone removed and cut into 5 cm (2 inch) batons

Pickled ginger, wasabi and gluten-free salt-reduced soy sauce, to serve (see tip)

SPICY SESAME CHICKEN

¼ teaspoon dried red chilli flakes

1 garlic clove, crushed

2 tablespoons gluten-free salt-reduced soy sauce

1 tablespoon sesame oil

2 (about 250 g/9 oz in total) skinless chicken thigh fillets, fat trimmed

1 To make the spicy sesame chicken, put the chilli flakes, garlic, soy sauce and sesame oil in a shallow glass or ceramic container. Add the chicken and stir to coat, then cover and put in the refrigerator for at least 1 hour to marinate.

2 Meanwhile, put the rice in a large saucepan with 750 ml (3 cups) cold water and bring to the boil. Reduce the heat to low, cover and simmer for 30–35 minutes, until all the water is absorbed. Remove from the heat, cover and set aside for 5 minutes. Add the seasoned rice vinegar to the rice and stir until well combined. Cover a large baking tray with foil, then spread the rice evenly over the tray and set aside to cool completely.

3 Meanwhile, heat a chargrill pan or non-stick frying pan over high heat and cook the chicken for 3–4 minutes each side, until golden and cooked through. Remove and set aside to cool, then cut into 1 cm (½ inch) thick slices.

4 Combine the white vinegar and 250 ml (1 cup) cold water in a small bowl. Divide the rice into 4 portions. Place a sheet of nori, shiny side down, on a bamboo mat. Dip your hands in the vinegar mixture, then spread one portion of the rice evenly over the bottom two-thirds of the nori sheet, leaving a small border around the edge.

5 Place a few slices of chicken along the middle of the rice and top with some cucumber and avocado. Lift up the end of the mat closest to you and roll it over the ingredients to enclose, then keep rolling to make a complete roll. Continue with the remaining nori, rice and fillings. Wrap each roll tightly in plastic wrap and refrigerate for 30 minutes. Slice and serve with pickled ginger, wasabi and soy sauce.

tip Seasoned vinegar, pickled ginger and wasabi should be gluten free, but always check the label.

vegetarian

Fresh broad beans have a short season in spring, and they can be tricky to find. Frozen ones are a great substitute, and the nutritional difference is negligible. You will need to remove the tough skins from frozen beans, whereas very young fresh broad beans can be eaten in their pods, like green beans.

Bruschetta with broad beans and marinated capsicums

Preparation time: 15 minutes
Cooking time: 10 minutes
(plus 20 minutes steaming)
Serves 4

2 red capsicums (peppers), halved and seeded (see tip)

2 tablespoons coarsely chopped basil, plus extra leaves to garnish

1 tablespoon salted baby capers, rinsed, drained and chopped

2 teaspoons extra virgin olive oil

2 teaspoons red wine vinegar

250 g (1½ cups) podded fresh or frozen broad beans

75 g (⅓ cup) ricotta cheese, crumbled

8 slices gluten-free or wholegrain bread, toasted

Mint leaves, to garnish

1 Preheat the grill (broiler) to high. Place the capsicums on a baking tray. Grill until the skin blackens and blisters. Transfer to a large bowl, cover with plastic wrap and set aside to steam for 20 minutes. Carefully peel off the skin and discard. Cut the capsicums into 1 cm (½ inch) wide strips.

2 Put the chopped basil, capers, olive oil and vinegar in a large bowl. Add the capsicum and stir to coat. Season to taste with sea salt and freshly ground black pepper.

3 Cook the broad beans in a saucepan of boiling water for 3 minutes or until tender. Refresh under cold running water. Drain. Peel off the skins and discard.

4 Add the beans and ricotta to the capsicum and gently toss to combine. Spoon onto the toasted bread. Serve immediately, garnished with basil and mint leaves.

tip You could use purchased roasted or wood-fired capsicums; you'll need about 150 g (5½ oz).

vegetarian

Try serving these falafel wrapped in gluten-free or wholegrain flatbread with tabouleh, or break them into chunks and toss them through a salad for a healthy and filling vegetarian meal. Chickpeas are a wonderful vegetarian source of protein and packed with insoluble fibre – great for digestive health.

Falafel with tomato and radish salad

Preparation time: 20 minutes (plus 30 minutes chilling)
Cooking time: 15 minutes
Serves 4

- **2 x 400 g (14 oz) cans chickpeas, drained and rinsed (see tip)**
- **⅓ cup mint leaves, coarsely chopped**
- **⅓ cup flat-leaf (Italian) parsley leaves, coarsely chopped**
- **1½ tablespoons toasted pine nuts**
- **1 egg white**
- **1 garlic clove, crushed**
- **1½ teaspoons ground cumin**
- **1 teaspoon ground coriander**
- **½ teaspoon bicarbonate of soda (baking soda)**
- **Gluten-free or wholemeal plain (all-purpose) flour, for dusting**
- **1 tablespoon extra virgin olive oil**
- **Natural yoghurt, to serve**
- **Grilled gluten-free or wholegrain flatbread, to serve**

TOMATO AND RADISH SALAD

- **200 g (7 oz) grape tomatoes, halved**
- **4 radishes, trimmed and thinly sliced**
- **¼ cup mint leaves**
- **3 spring onions (scallions), trimmed and thinly sliced**
- **2 teaspoons extra virgin olive oil**

1 Process the chickpeas, mint, parsley, pine nuts, egg white, garlic, spices and bicarbonate of soda in a food processor until almost smooth. Dust your hands with flour and shape the mixture into 20 small oval falafels. Place on a tray, cover with plastic wrap and refrigerate for 30 minutes to firm.

2 Meanwhile, to make the tomato and radish salad, combine the tomatoes, radishes, mint and spring onions in a bowl. Drizzle with the olive oil, season to taste with sea salt and freshly ground black pepper, and toss gently to combine. Set aside.

3 Heat the oil in a large non-stick frying pan over medium–high heat. Cook the falafels, in two batches, for 4 minutes each side or until golden brown and cooked through. Serve with the tomato and radish salad, yoghurt and flatbread.

tip You can replace the canned chickpeas with 450 g (2⅔ cups) cooked chickpeas.

vegetarian

This salad is a great multi-tasker: it's delicious served as a starter, lunch, light dinner, or even as a breakfast dish.

Chickpea, zucchini and mint salad

Preparation time: 15 minutes
Cooking time: 5 minutes
Serves 4

2 large zucchini (courgettes), trimmed
2 teaspoons white balsamic vinegar
2 teaspoons extra virgin olive oil
2 teaspoons finely grated lemon zest
400 g (14 oz) can chickpeas, drained and rinsed (see tips)
100 g (3½ oz) roasted red capsicum (pepper), thinly sliced (see tips)
¼ cup baby or micro mint leaves
4 poached eggs
75 g (⅓ cup) ricotta cheese, crumbled
Grilled gluten-free or wholegrain bread, to serve (optional)

1 Peel long ribbons from the zucchini using a vegetable peeler, stopping when you reach the seeds. Place the zucchini ribbons in a large bowl (discard the seeds or reserve for another use) and add the vinegar, olive oil and lemon zest. Set aside to marinate for 5 minutes.

2 Add the chickpeas, capsicum and half the mint and toss to combine. Divide the salad among four plates. Top each with a poached egg, sprinkle with ricotta, garnish with the remaining mint and serve with the grilled bread, if using.

tips You can replace the canned chickpeas with 225 g (1⅓ cups) cooked chickpeas.

To roast your own capsicum, cut a large capsicum in half and remove the seeds and membranes. Put the halves on a baking tray and roast at 200°C (400°F) for 20–25 minutes, or until the skin starts to blacken. Transfer to a small bowl, cover with plastic wrap and set aside to steam for 15 minutes. Carefully peel off the skin and discard.

D

vegetarian

I love adding quinoa flakes to baked goods, such as these muffins. They taste great and also add protein, calcium, iron and B vitamins, making them the perfect addition to healthy lunch boxes.

Quinoa, feta, roasted capsicum and corn muffins

Preparation time: 20 minutes
Cooking time: 20 minutes
Makes 12

- **225 g (1½ cups) gluten-free or wholemeal self-raising flour**
- **110 g (1 cup) quinoa flakes**
- **200 g (1 cup) corn kernels (fresh, canned or frozen)**
- **120 g (4¼ oz) drained roasted capsicum (pepper) in oil, diced**
- **75 g (2¾ oz) reduced-fat feta cheese, crumbled**
- **2 tablespoons snipped chives**
- **250 ml (1 cup) reduced-fat milk**
- **1 egg**
- **80 ml (⅓ cup) macadamia oil**

1 Preheat the oven to 180°C (350°F). Line a 12-hole 80 ml (⅓ cup) muffin tin with paper cases.

2 Sift the flour into a large bowl and stir in the quinoa flakes, corn, capsicum, feta and chives. Combine the milk, egg and oil in a large jug, add to the dry ingredients and stir until well combined (do not over-mix).

3 Divide the mixture among the lined muffin holes and bake for 20 minutes or until golden and cooked through. Set aside for 5 minutes to cool, then transfer to a wire rack. Serve warm or at room temperature.

tip These muffins can be wrapped well in plastic wrap and frozen for up to 1 month. Thaw at room temperature.

salads

dairy free

This flavoursome salad is similar to a tabouleh, but unlike the traditional cracked wheat version it is gluten free. Buckwheat is rich in rutin, a phytonutrient believed to lower cholesterol and reduce blood pressure.

Buckwheat and grilled chicken summer salad

Preparation time: 20 minutes
(plus 30 minutes marinating)
Cooking time: 25 minutes
Serves 4

60 ml (1/4 cup) lemon juice
60 ml (1/4 cup) extra virgin olive oil
2 garlic cloves, crushed
500 g (1 lb 2 oz) skinless chicken thigh fillets, fat trimmed
200 g (1 cup) raw buckwheat
1 Lebanese (short) cucumber, trimmed and diced
250 g (9 oz) mixed cherry and grape tomatoes, halved or quartered depending on size
1/4 cup flat-leaf (Italian) parsley leaves
1/4 cup mint leaves, torn
1/4 cup basil leaves, torn
4 spring onions (scallions), trimmed and thinly sliced
1 teaspoon sumac (see tips), plus extra, to garnish

1 Put half the lemon juice, half the oil and the garlic in a shallow glass or ceramic container and stir to combine. Add the chicken and stir to coat. Cover and set aside for 30 minutes to marinate.

2 Meanwhile, heat a large non-stick frying pan over medium–high heat. Add the buckwheat and cook, stirring, for 3–4 minutes or until fragrant. Put the toasted buckwheat and 500 ml (2 cups) water in a saucepan and bring to the boil. Cover, reduce the heat to low and simmer for 10–12 minutes or until just tender (be careful not to overcook). Rinse under cold running water, then drain well.

3 Transfer the drained buckwheat to a large mixing bowl and add the cucumber, tomatoes, herbs, spring onions, sumac and the remaining lemon juice and olive oil. Stir to combine, then season with sea salt and freshly ground black pepper.

4 Preheat a chargrill pan over medium–high heat. Cook the chicken for 4 minutes each side or until lightly charred and cooked through. Set aside to cool slightly, then thinly slice. Add the chicken to the salad and toss to combine. Serve sprinkled with a little extra sumac.

tips Sumac is a spice used in Mediterranean and Middle Eastern cooking. It has a tangy citrus flavour and a vibrant, deep red colour.

Toasting the buckwheat before cooking only takes a few minutes, but it results in a much better flavour. I find toasting it myself is better than buying commercial toasted buckwheat (known as kasha), as it can be very dark in colour and overpowering in taste.

vegan (see tips)

Broccoli is a true superfood, packed with disease- and cancer-fighting compounds and rich in vitamin C, beta-carotene, folate, iron and potassium. Broccoli is also rich in a compound called sulforaphane, which may assist in the prevention and treatment of osteoarthritis.

Roasted broccoli and chickpea salad with herbed tahini dressing

Preparation time: 15 minutes
Cooking time: 20 minutes
Serves 4

½ cauliflower, cut into florets

Extra virgin olive oil spray

300 g (10½ oz) broccoli, cut into florets

¼ cup chopped flat-leaf (Italian) parsley

2 tablespoons lemon juice

2 teaspoons extra virgin olive oil

1 teaspoon garam masala

255 g (1½ cups) drained cooked chickpeas (see tips)

4 spring onions (scallions), thinly sliced

1 tablespoon unhulled tahini (see tips)

1 teaspoon single origin floral honey (see tips)

1½ tablespoons pine nuts, lightly toasted

1 Preheat the oven to 180°C (350°F). Line a large baking tray with baking paper. Place the cauliflower on the tray, spray lightly with olive oil and roast for 10 minutes. Add the broccoli, spray lightly and roast for a further 10 minutes or until golden and tender.

2 Meanwhile, combine 2 tablespoons of the parsley with 1 tablespoon of the lemon juice, the olive oil and the garam masala in a large bowl. Stir in the chickpeas and spring onions and leave for 5 minutes.

3 Combine the tahini, remaining parsley, remaining lemon juice, honey and 1–2 tablespoons warm water to make a thin dressing.

4 Stir the broccoli and cauliflower into the chickpea mixture. Pile the salad onto a plate, drizzle with the dressing and sprinkle with the pine nuts.

tips For a vegan version, replace the honey with pure maple syrup.

You can replace the cooked chickpeas with a 400 g (14 oz) can of chickpeas.

Unhulled tahini is made from whole sesame seeds and is more nutritious than hulled tahini. Look for it in the health-food section of your supermarket.

vegan

The sweet potato and quinoa give this salad a low GI rating. If you have any leftovers, take them to work for a lunch that will provide slow-release energy throughout the day.

Spiced quinoa, sweet potato, broccoli and cranberry salad

Preparation time: 20 minutes
Cooking time: 25–30 minutes
Serves 4

700 g (1 lb 9 oz) orange sweet potato, peeled and cut into 1.5 cm (5/8 inch) dice

60 ml (1/4 cup) extra virgin olive oil

200 g (1 cup) quinoa (see tip), briefly rinsed

1/2 teaspoon ground turmeric

1 teaspoon ground cumin

250 g (9 oz) broccoli, trimmed and cut into small florets

1 bunch asparagus, trimmed and cut into 2 cm (3/4 inch) lengths

50 g (1/3 cup) sweetened dried cranberries

1/3 cup coarsely chopped mixed herbs (such as chives, parsley, mint)

2 tablespoons fresh orange juice

1 tablespoon white balsamic vinegar

1 Preheat the oven to 200°C (400°F). Place the sweet potato on a large baking tray lined with baking paper. Drizzle with 1 tablespoon of the olive oil and season with sea salt and pepper. Roast for 25–30 minutes or until golden and tender.

2 Meanwhile, put the quinoa, turmeric, cumin and 500 ml (2 cups) water in a saucepan and bring to the boil. Reduce the heat to low, cover and simmer for 12 minutes or until the water is absorbed. Remove from the heat and set aside to cool slightly.

3 Blanch the broccoli and asparagus in a saucepan of boiling water until tender-crisp, then drain and refresh under cold running water.

4 Put the cooked quinoa, sweet potato, blanched vegetables, cranberries and herbs in a large bowl. Whisk together the remaining 2 tablespoons of olive oil, the orange juice and vinegar. Add to the salad and toss to combine, then season with sea salt and freshly ground black pepper, to taste.

tip I used equal quantities of red and white quinoa in this recipe. There is no need to cook them separately.

vegan (see tips)

I absolutely love raw beetroot in salads, especially when it's teamed with nutty puy lentils and lots of chopped herbs for freshness. Beetroot is a good source of folate and is rich in the plant pigments betacyanins, with potential anti-inflammatory properties.

Raw beetroot and lentil salad with mustard dressing

Preparation time: 15 minutes
Cooking time: 25 minutes
Serves 4

- 160 g (3/4 cup) puy lentils, rinsed
- 2 teaspoons extra virgin olive oil
- 1 red onion, finely chopped
- 2 celery stalks, finely chopped
- 400 g (14 oz/about 3) beetroot (beets), coarsely grated (see tips)
- 1 tablespoon flaxseed or extra virgin olive oil
- 1 tablespoon balsamic vinegar
- 2 teaspoons wholegrain mustard (see tips)
- 1 teaspoon single origin floral honey (see tips)
- 2 tablespoons chopped flat-leaf (Italian) parsley
- 2 tablespoons chopped mint

1 Cook the lentils in a saucepan of boiling water for 20–25 minutes or until just tender. Refresh under cold running water and drain well.

2 Meanwhile, heat the olive oil in a large non-stick frying pan over medium heat. Add the onion and cook, stirring, for 5 minutes or until softened. Remove from the heat and add the lentils, celery and beetroot.

3 Whisk together the flaxseed oil, vinegar, mustard and honey. Pour the dressing over the lentil mixture, add the parsley and mint and toss gently. Season to taste with sea salt and freshly ground black pepper.

tips When you're handling the beetroot, wear gloves so your hands don't become stained.

For a vegan version, replace the honey with pure maple syrup.

Wholegrain mustard should be gluten-free, but always check the label.

This salad will keep in an airtight container in the refrigerator for up to 2 days.

dairy free

Amaranth grain is naturally gluten free and rich in manganese, iron, magnesium and phosphorus. It is also packed with dietary fibre and is a great vegetable source of protein. It becomes slightly sticky when cooked so it is best combined with quinoa when used as a salad grain.

Grain salad with salmon, red grapes and watercress

Preparation time: 20 minutes (plus cooling)
Cooking time: 20 minutes
Serves 4

- 200 g (1 cup) Andean grain mix (see tips), briefly rinsed
- 2 x 200 g (7 oz) skinless salmon fillets
- 2 tablespoons extra virgin olive oil, plus 2 teaspoons, extra
- 250 g (9 oz) sugar snap peas, trimmed
- 200 g (7 oz) seedless red grapes, halved
- 60 g (2 cups) picked watercress sprigs (see tips), washed
- ¼ cup snipped chives
- 1½ tablespoons lemon juice
- 1 teaspoon finely grated lemon zest
- ½ teaspoon pure maple syrup (optional)

1 Put the grain mix in a saucepan with 500 ml (2 cups) water and bring to the boil. Reduce the heat to low, cover and simmer for 12 minutes or until the water is absorbed. Remove from the heat and set aside to cool completely.

2 Brush the salmon fillets with the extra olive oil. Heat a non-stick frying pan over high heat and cook the salmon for 2–3 minutes each side (for medium) or until cooked to your liking. Remove and set aside to cool slightly, then break up the salmon into large flakes.

3 Blanch the sugar snap peas in a saucepan of boiling water until they are tender-crisp. Drain and refresh under cold running water.

4 Put the cooked grain mix, salmon, sugar snaps, grapes, watercress and chives in a large bowl. Whisk the olive oil, lemon juice, zest and maple syrup (if using) together. Add to the salad and gently toss to combine, then season with sea salt and freshly ground black pepper to taste.

tips Andean grain mix is also sometimes called 'supergrain mix' and is a combination of amaranth and red, white and black quinoa. To make your own, simply combine equal quantities of these grains.

You can replace the watercress with baby rocket (arugula) or baby spinach leaves if you like.

vegan (see tips)

I love using wholegrain brown rice in salads as it gives so much flavour and texture. Sunflower seeds also give added crunch, as well as being a good source of the anti-inflammatory antioxidant vitamin E.

Rice salad with roasted pumpkin, beans and orange spice dressing

Preparation time: 25 minutes
Cooking time: 30 minutes
Serves 4

800 g (1 lb 12 oz) pumpkin (winter squash), peeled, seeded and cut into 1.5 cm (5/8 inch) cubes

1 tablespoon extra virgin olive oil

250 g (9 oz) green beans, trimmed and cut into 3 cm (1¼ inch) lengths

585 g (3 cups) cooked medium-grain brown rice, cooled

1 zucchini (courgette), trimmed, halved and thinly sliced

40 g (¼ cup) sunflower seeds

¼ cup flat-leaf (Italian) parsley leaves, coarsely chopped

¼ cup mint leaves, shredded

ORANGE SPICE DRESSING

80 ml (⅓ cup) freshly squeezed orange juice

2 tablespoons extra virgin olive oil

3 teaspoons white wine vinegar

1 teaspoon single origin floral honey

½ teaspoon ground cinnamon

1½ teaspoons ground cumin

1 Preheat the oven to 200°C (400°F). Put the pumpkin on a large baking tray lined with baking paper. Season with sea salt and freshly ground black pepper and drizzle with the olive oil. Roast for 25–30 minutes, until the pumpkin is golden and tender.

2 Meanwhile, blanch the beans in a saucepan of boiling water until bright green and tender-crisp. Refresh under cold running water, then drain well.

3 Put the roasted pumpkin, beans, rice, zucchini, sunflower seeds, parsley and mint in a large bowl and stir to combine.

4 To make the dressing, put all the ingredients in a small bowl and whisk to combine. Add to the salad and stir to combine. Season with sea salt and freshly ground black pepper, to taste.

tips For a vegan version, replace the honey with pure maple syrup.

This salad will keep, covered, in the refrigerator for up to 2 days.

vegetarian

The earthy flavour of the buckwheat is delicious with roasted beetroot. Buckwheat is an ideal grain for vegetarian dishes such as this, as it is rich in protein, B vitamins, calcium and phosphorus. The hazelnuts also add extra protein, fibre, vitamin E – and crunch.

Roasted beetroot and buckwheat salad

Preparation time: 20 minutes (plus cooling)
Cooking time: 45 minutes
Serves 4

10–12 (about 600 g/1 lb 5 oz in total) baby beetroot (beets), trimmed

200 g (1 cup) raw buckwheat

75 g (½ cup) hazelnuts, lightly toasted and skinned

100 g (3½ oz) baby rocket (arugula) leaves

2 tablespoons snipped chives

100 g (½ cup) ricotta cheese, crumbled (optional)

DRESSING

2 tablespoons walnut oil

2 tablespoons fresh orange juice

1 tablespoon balsamic vinegar

1 Preheat the oven to 200°C (400°F). Put the beetroot in a large roasting pan, cover the pan with foil and roast for 40–45 minutes or until they are tender when pierced with a skewer. Set aside to cool slightly, then peel (see tips) and cut into wedges.

2 Meanwhile, heat a large non-stick frying pan over medium–high heat. Add the buckwheat and cook, stirring, for 3–4 minutes or until fragrant. Put the toasted buckwheat and 500 ml (2 cups) water in a saucepan and bring to the boil. Cover, reduce the heat to low and simmer for 10–12 minutes or until just tender (be careful not to overcook). Rinse under cold running water, then drain well.

3 Coarsely chop the hazelnuts and place in a large bowl. Add the beetroot, cooked buckwheat, rocket and chives and stir to combine.

4 To make the dressing, whisk the walnut oil, orange juice and vinegar in a small bowl until combined. Add to the salad and toss well. Sprinkle with the ricotta cheese, if using, and season with sea salt and freshly ground black pepper, to taste.

tip Wear gloves while peeling the beetroot to prevent your hands becoming stained by the juices.

dairy free

Buttery and almost corn-like, millet is a good match with Mexican flavours such as lime, chilli and coriander. Millet is relatively quick to cook, gluten free and has a lovely al dente texture once cooked.

Millet salad with chilli lime prawns

Preparation time: 20 minutes (plus cooling)
Cooking time: 40 minutes
Serves 4

½ teaspoon dried red chilli flakes

2 teaspoons finely grated lime zest

2 tablespoons extra virgin olive oil

20 large raw prawns (shrimp), peeled and deveined with tails left intact

210 g (1 cup) hulled millet

2 large corn cobs

1 bunch asparagus, trimmed and halved

1 firm ripe avocado, peeled, stone removed and diced

½ cup coriander (cilantro) leaves, coarsely chopped

Lime wedges, to serve

DRESSING

2 tablespoons lime juice

2 tablespoons extra virgin olive oil

1 long red chilli, seeded and finely chopped

½ teaspoon pure maple syrup (optional)

1 Put the chilli flakes, lime zest and 1 tablespoon of the olive oil in a shallow glass or ceramic bowl. Add the prawns and stir to coat, then cover and set aside.

2 Heat a large saucepan over medium–high heat, add the millet and cook, stirring, for 3 minutes or until fragrant.

3 Add 500 ml (2 cups) water to the millet and bring to the boil. Reduce the heat to low, cover and simmer for 15–20 minutes or until the water is absorbed. Remove from the heat and set aside, covered, to steam for 10 minutes. Fluff the grains with a fork and transfer to a large bowl to cool completely.

4 Heat a large chargrill pan over high heat. Drizzle the corn and asparagus with the remaining oil. Cook the corn, turning, for 6–8 minutes or until lightly charred and tender. Remove and set aside to cool slightly, then cut the kernels from the cobs. Cook the asparagus and prawns for 2 minutes each side or until the asparagus is tender-crisp and the prawns are just cooked through. Set the prawns aside. Add the asparagus, corn kernels, avocado and coriander to the millet.

5 To make the dressing, put all the ingredients in a small bowl and whisk until well combined. Add to the salad and toss gently to combine. Season with sea salt and freshly ground black pepper, to taste.

6 To serve, divide the salad among serving plates, top with the chargrilled prawns and serve with lime wedges.

vegan (see tips)

Peanuts are rich in the antioxidant resveratrol, which has been linked to a reduced risk of cardiovascular disease. They're also a good source of niacin, folate and vitamin E with anti-inflammatory properties.

Brown rice salad with peanuts

Preparation time: 15 minutes
Cooking time: 25 minutes
Serves 4

220 g (1 cup) brown rice

150 g (5½ oz) snow peas (mangetout), trimmed and thinly sliced

200 g (7 oz) grape tomatoes, halved

70 g (½ cup) unsalted roasted peanuts, coarsely chopped

4 spring onions (scallions), trimmed and thinly sliced

2 tablespoons currants

2 tablespoons coarsely chopped flat-leaf (Italian) parsley

2 tablespoons coarsely chopped mint

DRESSING

1½ tablespoons extra virgin olive oil

1 tablespoon balsamic vinegar

1 tablespoon lemon juice

½ teaspoon single origin floral honey (optional)

1 Cook the brown rice in a large saucepan of boiling water according to the packet instructions or until just tender. Drain, transfer to a large bowl and set aside.

2 Put the snow peas in a heatproof bowl. Pour over enough boiling water to cover, then set aside to blanch for 30 seconds. Refresh under cold running water. Drain and add to the rice. Add the tomatoes, peanuts, spring onions, currants, parsley and mint.

3 To make the dressing, whisk the olive oil, vinegar, lemon juice and honey, if using, in a small bowl until well combined.

4 Drizzle the dressing over the salad and gently toss to combine, then serve.

tips For a vegan version, replace the honey with pure maple syrup.

This salad will keep in an airtight container in the refrigerator for up to 3 days. Bring it to room temperature before serving.

vegan

Different coloured vegetables all provide something unique nutritionally, so aim to eat a serving from each colour group every day. This multi-hued salad is brimming with disease-fighting phytonutrients.

Rainbow slaw

Preparation time: 15 minutes
Cooking time: None
Serves 4–6

½ small red cabbage, shredded

2 carrots, cut into thin matchsticks

100 g (3½ oz) sugar snap peas, thinly sliced

100 g (3½ oz) snow peas (mangetout), thinly sliced

1 red capsicum (pepper), thinly sliced

2 tablespoons chopped mint

2 tablespoons chopped flat-leaf (Italian) parsley

2 tablespoons sultanas, coarsely chopped

1 tablespoon lemon juice

1 tablespoon flaxseed or extra virgin olive oil

2 tablespoons unsalted roasted cashews, chopped

1 Combine the vegetables, herbs and sultanas in a large bowl.

2 Whisk together the lemon juice and flaxseed oil, add the dressing to the salad and toss gently. Serve garnished with chopped cashews.

vegan (see tips)

Borlotti beans have a creamy rich texture and nutty flavour that is a perfect match with the honey-roasted pumpkin and anti-inflammatory hazelnuts. They are also nutritious, being high in protein and fibre.

Honey-roasted pumpkin, borlotti bean, broccolini and hazelnut salad

Preparation time: 15 minutes
Cooking time: 40 minutes
Serves 4

1½ tablespoons single origin floral honey

1½ tablespoons extra virgin olive oil

2 teaspoons coarsely chopped rosemary

800 g (1 lb 12 oz) pumpkin (winter squash), seeded and cut into wedges (see tips)

2 teaspoons red wine vinegar

250 g (9 oz/about 2 bunches) broccolini, trimmed

400 g (14 oz) can borlotti beans, drained and rinsed (see tips)

1 head radicchio, trimmed and leaves torn

2 tablespoons lightly toasted hazelnuts, coarsely chopped

1 Preheat the oven to 200°C (400°F). Line a large baking tray with baking paper. Combine 1 tablespoon of the honey, 1 tablespoon of the olive oil and the rosemary in a large bowl. Add the pumpkin and toss to coat. Place on the tray and roast for 30–40 minutes or until golden, turning halfway through the cooking time.

2 Meanwhile, combine the remaining honey and oil with the vinegar in a small bowl. Set aside.

3 Cook the broccolini in a saucepan of boiling water until just tender. Drain.

4 Combine the pumpkin, broccolini, borlotti beans, radicchio and hazelnuts in a large bowl. Add the honey dressing and gently toss to combine. Season to taste with sea salt and freshly ground black pepper.

tips For a vegan version, replace the honey with pure maple syrup.

Queensland blue pumpkin has a firm texture after roasting, so it's ideal to use in this salad. Butternut pumpkin (squash) is a good substitute.

You can replace the canned borlotti beans with 255 g (1½ cups) cooked borlotti beans.

vegan

Quinoa and kale give this version of tabouleh a gluten-free modern twist. Kale is loaded with vitamin C, which assists immunity; beta-carotene, which is essential for eye health; and antioxidants, which help protect against cancer. Toasted pepitas add a delicious crunch and monounsaturated fatty acids.

Kale, quinoa and mint tabouleh

Preparation time: 20 minutes
Cooking time: 15 minutes
Serves 4

- **100 g (½ cup) quinoa, rinsed and drained**
- **300 g (10 ½ oz, about ½ bunch) kale, centre vein removed**
- **Extra virgin olive oil spray**
- **200 g (7 oz) grape tomatoes, chopped**
- **2 Lebanese (short) cucumbers, seeded and diced**
- **¼ cup mint leaves, chopped**
- **¼ cup flat-leaf (Italian) parsley leaves, chopped**
- **2 tablespoons pepitas (pumpkin seeds), lightly toasted**
- **40 g (1½ oz) pitted dates, finely chopped**
- **1 tablespoon lemon juice**
- **1 tablespoon flaxseed or extra virgin olive oil**

1 Put the quinoa and 250 ml (1 cup) cold water in a saucepan. Bring to the boil, cover, reduce the heat to low and simmer for 12 minutes or until the water has evaporated and the quinoa is al dente. Set aside to cool completely.

2 Meanwhile, preheat the oven to 200°C (400°F) and line a baking tray with baking paper. Tear the kale into bite-size pieces, place in a single layer on the tray and spray with olive oil. Bake for 8–10 minutes or until crisp and golden. Season to taste with sea salt and leave to cool completely.

3 Toss half the kale with the quinoa, tomatoes, cucumber, mint, parsley, pepitas and dates in a large bowl. Whisk together the lemon juice and flaxseed oil, add the dressing to the salad and toss well. Season to taste and serve topped with the remaining crisp kale.

vegetarian

Regular peas are eaten without their pods, whereas sugar snaps and snow peas are eaten whole, pods included. This salad makes the most of their crisp texture and fresh taste. Buttermilk, despite its name, is low in fat, but it has a lovely creamy texture and a slight tang, making it perfect for a salad dressing.

Three-pea salad with buttermilk herb dressing

Preparation time: 15 minutes
Cooking time: 5 minutes
Serves 4

140 g (1 cup) podded fresh or frozen baby peas

200 g (7 oz) snow peas (mangetout), trimmed

200 g (7 oz) sugar snap peas, trimmed

4 small radishes, trimmed and thinly sliced

¼ cup mint leaves

¼ cup flat-leaf (Italian) parsley leaves

BUTTERMILK HERB DRESSING

60 ml (¼ cup) buttermilk

1 tablespoon finely snipped chives

1 tablespoon finely chopped dill or flat-leaf (Italian) parsley

2 teaspoons lemon juice

1 teaspoon finely grated lemon zest

1 Put the baby peas in a steamer over a saucepan of boiling water, cover and steam for 3–4 minutes or until just tender. Refresh under cold running water, drain and transfer to a large bowl. Steam the snow peas and sugar snap peas in the same way, cooking for 2 minutes or until just tender. Refresh, drain and transfer to the bowl with the baby peas. Add the radishes, mint and parsley and toss gently to combine.

2 To make the buttermilk herb dressing, whisk all the ingredients in a small bowl until combined.

3 Arrange the salad on a serving platter and drizzle with the dressing. Serve immediately.

soups & curries

vegan

The kidney beans give this pumpkin soup body and a delicious thick texture. Red kidney beans, like all legumes, contain various phytochemicals that help to protect against cancer, heart disease and have potential anti-inflammatory properties.

Pumpkin, bean and coconut soup

Preparation time: 15 minutes
Cooking time: 30 minutes
Serves 4

1 tablespoon extra virgin olive oil
1 large onion, coarsely chopped
2 celery stalks, trimmed and diced
2 garlic cloves, crushed
2 teaspoons finely grated ginger
2 teaspoons curry powder
1 kg (2 lb 4 oz) pumpkin (winter squash), peeled, seeded and coarsely chopped
1 litre (4 cups) homemade or salt-reduced gluten-free vegetable stock
400 g (14 oz) can red kidney beans or pinto beans, drained and rinsed
80 ml (1/3 cup) reduced-fat coconut milk, plus extra to serve
Lime juice, to taste
Toasted coconut flakes, to garnish
Coriander (cilantro) leaves, to garnish

1 Heat the olive oil in a large saucepan over medium heat. Add the onion and celery and cook, stirring, for 6–7 minutes or until softened. Add the garlic, ginger and curry powder and cook, stirring, for 1 minute or until fragrant.

2 Add the pumpkin and stock. Bring to the boil, then reduce the heat to low and simmer, partially covered, for 10 minutes. Add the beans and simmer for 5–10 minutes or until the pumpkin is tender. Set aside to cool slightly.

3 Blend the soup, in batches, in a blender until smooth and creamy. Return the soup to a clean saucepan and stir over medium heat until heated through. Stir in the coconut milk and season to taste with sea salt, freshly ground black pepper and lime juice.

4 Serve drizzled with extra coconut milk and garnished with toasted coconut flakes and coriander.

tip This soup is suitable to freeze. Put it in airtight containers and cool completely. Cover and freeze for up to 2 months.

vegetarian

This soup is perfect for vegetarians, as combining legumes (chickpeas) with a whole grain such as quinoa makes a complete protein and therefore a balanced meal.

Chickpea, tomato and quinoa soup with pesto toasts

Preparation time: 20 minutes
Cooking time: 35 minutes
Serves 4

1 tablespoon extra virgin olive oil

1 large red onion, finely chopped

1 large celery stalk, diced

2 garlic cloves, crushed

1 long red chilli, seeded and finely chopped

1 teaspoon ground cumin

2 teaspoons sweet paprika

1 tablespoon no-added-salt tomato paste (concentrated purée)

400 g (14 oz) can chickpeas, drained and rinsed

65 g (1/3 cup) quinoa (see tips), briefly rinsed

400 g (14 oz) can chopped tomatoes

750 ml (3 cups) homemade or salt-reduced gluten-free vegetable stock

4 slices gluten-free or wholegrain bread

Basil pesto, to serve

1 Heat the oil in a large saucepan over medium heat and cook the onion and celery, stirring, for 5–6 minutes or until soft. Add the garlic, chilli and spices and cook, stirring, for 1 minute, then add the tomato paste and cook, stirring, for 1 minute more.

2 Add the chickpeas, quinoa, tomatoes and stock and bring to the boil. Reduce the heat to low, partially cover and simmer for 25 minutes.

3 Blend half the soup until smooth and return to the saucepan with the remaining soup. Season and reheat gently.

4 Meanwhile, toast the bread until golden and then spread with a little basil pesto. Serve the pesto toasts with the soup.

tips You can use either white or red quinoa in this recipe.

This soup freezes well (without the pesto toasts). Simply place the cooled soup in airtight containers and freeze.

vegetarian

Beetroot has been used medicinally for centuries to help detoxify the liver. This soup, which combines beetroot with the natural aniseed flavour of fennel, is the perfect pick-me-up for when you're feeling sluggish. Beetroot's vibrant red-purple colour comes from betacyanins: plant pigments that act as powerful antioxidants.

Pick-me-up beetroot soup with spiced yoghurt

Preparation time: 20 minutes
Cooking time: 1 hour 30 minutes
Serves 4

1 kg (2 lb 4 oz/about 5 large) beetroot, scrubbed
1 tablespoon extra virgin olive oil
1 leek, thinly sliced
1 small fennel bulb, chopped
3 celery stalks, diced
2 garlic cloves, crushed
1 teaspoon fennel seeds, crushed
750 ml (3 cups) homemade or salt-reduced gluten-free vegetable stock
130 g (½ cup) natural yoghurt
½ teaspoon ground cumin
½ teaspoon ground coriander
Mint leaves, to garnish

1 Preheat the oven to 200°C (400°F). Place the beetroot in a large roasting tin and cover with foil. Roast for 1 hour or until tender when pierced with a skewer. Cool, then peel and chop.

2 Heat the oil in a large saucepan over medium heat. Add the leek, chopped fennel and celery and cook, stirring, for 6–7 minutes or until softened. Add the garlic and fennel seeds and stir for 1 minute or until fragrant.

3 Add the stock and beetroot and bring to the boil. Reduce the heat and simmer, partially covered, for 20 minutes. Blend the soup in batches, then reheat gently.

4 Stir together the yoghurt, cumin and coriander. Serve the soup with a dollop of spiced yoghurt and a sprinkle of mint.

tip The soup can be frozen in airtight containers for up to 2 months.

(pictured page 87)

vegan

Celeriac might be ugly on the outside, but beneath its lumpy surface the creamy white flesh of this large winter root vegetable has a unique mild celery flavour. Combined with leek and potato, it makes a deliciously smooth soup that is perfect for a cold night.

Celeriac and leek soup with hazelnuts and crisp sage

Preparation time: 20 minutes
Cooking time: 30 minutes
Serves 4

40 g (1/4 cup) hazelnuts

1½ tablespoons extra virgin olive oil

1 leek, white part only, thinly sliced

2 garlic cloves, crushed

1 litre (4 cups) homemade or salt-reduced gluten-free vegetable stock

1 celeriac (about 650 g/1 lb 7 oz), chopped

500 g (1 lb 2 oz) floury potatoes, such as russet burbank or sebago, chopped

24 small sage leaves

1 Preheat the oven to 180°C (350°F). Spread the hazelnuts on a baking tray and lightly toast for 10 minutes. Wrap the nuts in a tea towel and rub off the skins. Cool, then chop coarsely.

2 Heat 1 tablespoon of the oil in a large saucepan over medium–low heat. Cook the leek, stirring, for 6–7 minutes until softened. Add the garlic and stir for 1 minute or until aromatic.

3 Add the stock, celeriac and potato and bring to the boil. Reduce the heat to low and simmer, partially covered, for 20 minutes or until very tender. Leave to cool slightly.

4 Blend the soup in batches until smooth, then reheat gently. Season to taste.

5 Meanwhile, heat the remaining oil in a frying pan over medium heat and fry the sage leaves for 1–2 minutes until crisp. Drain on paper towel.

6 Serve the soup with the toasted hazelnuts and sage leaves.

tip The soup can be frozen in airtight containers for up to 2 months.

(pictured page 87)

Pick-me-up beetroot soup with spiced yoghurt

(see recipe page 84)

Celeriac and leek soup with hazelnuts and crisp sage

(see recipe page 85)

dairy free

Black beans contain the winning combo of high protein and high fibre. Their distinctive black coating is also rich in anthocyanins – these pigments (also found in blueberries) have a powerful antioxidant effect that may help reduce inflammation and prevent cancer and heart disease.

Prawn and black bean soup with lime

Preparation time: 20 minutes (plus overnight soaking)
Cooking time: 1 hour 20 minutes
Serves 4 as a light meal

165 g (¾ cup) dried black beans, soaked overnight in cold water and drained (see tips)

2 teaspoons extra virgin olive oil

1 red onion, finely chopped

2 celery stalks, diced

3 garlic cloves, crushed

1 chipotle pepper in adobo sauce, finely chopped (see tips)

2 teaspoons paprika

1 teaspoon ground cumin

Pinch of cayenne pepper

2 tablespoons chopped coriander (cilantro) leaves

3 large vine-ripened tomatoes, diced

750 ml (3 cups) homemade or salt-reduced gluten-free vegetable or chicken stock

400 g (14 oz) peeled raw prawns (shrimp), tails intact

1 tablespoon lime juice, plus lime wedges to serve

Sliced avocado, to garnish

1 Put the black beans in a large saucepan, add enough cold water to cover them by 5 cm (2 inches) and bring to the boil. Reduce the heat to low and simmer for 45 minutes–1 hour until tender. Drain, rinse under cold running water and drain well.

2 Heat the olive oil in a large saucepan over medium heat. Add the onion and celery and cook, stirring, for 5 minutes or until softened. Add the garlic, chipotle, paprika, cumin, cayenne and coriander and cook, stirring, for 1 minute or until fragrant.

3 Add the tomatoes and cook for 1 minute, then add the stock and black beans and bring to the boil. Reduce the heat to low and simmer for 10 minutes. Add the prawns and simmer for 2–3 minutes or until the prawns are just cooked through. Add lime juice to taste and serve garnished with avocado, with lime wedges on the side.

tips You can replace the cooked dried beans with 350 g (2 cups) canned black beans, rinsed and drained.

Chipotle pepper in adobo sauce should be gluten-free, but always check the label.

vegan

Chickpeas make this soup extremely filling and nutritious. It's substantial enough to serve as a main meal.

Chickpea, lemon and silverbeet soup

Preparation time: 20 minutes
Cooking time: 30 minutes
Serves 4

1 tablespoon extra virgin olive oil
1 large onion, finely chopped
1 fennel bulb, finely chopped
2 celery stalks, diced
3 garlic cloves, crushed
1 teaspoon finely grated lemon zest
½ teaspoon dried chilli flakes
4 vine-ripened tomatoes, diced
2 x 400 g (14 oz) cans chickpeas, drained and rinsed (see tips)
1 litre (4 cups) homemade or salt-reduced gluten-free vegetable stock
100 g (3½ oz) trimmed and shredded silverbeet (Swiss chard) leaves (see tips)
Lemon juice, to taste

1 Heat the olive oil in a large saucepan over medium heat. Add the onion, fennel and celery and cook, stirring, for 6–7 minutes or until softened. Add the garlic, lemon zest and chilli flakes and cook, stirring, for 1 minute or until fragrant.

2 Add the tomatoes and cook, stirring, for 2–3 minutes. Add the chickpeas and stock and bring to the boil. Reduce the heat to low and simmer for 15 minutes.

3 Stir in the silverbeet and simmer for 2 minutes or until wilted. Season to taste with lemon juice, sea salt and freshly ground black pepper.

tips You can replace the canned chickpeas with 450 g (2⅔ cups) cooked chickpeas.

You'll need about half a bunch of silverbeet for this recipe.

This soup is suitable to freeze. Place it in airtight containers, cool completely, cover and freeze for up to 2 months.

vegan

Moong dal are skinned yellow split lentils with a sweet and nutty taste. They tend to break down quickly with cooking and are ideal for dishes that require thickening, such as dal.

Spinach and lentil dal

Preparation time: 15 minutes
Cooking time: 35 minutes
Serves 4

2 tablespoons macadamia oil
1 onion, finely chopped
220 g (1 cup) dried yellow split lentils (moong dal)
2 vine-ripened tomatoes, diced
Pinch cayenne pepper
1 teaspoon black mustard seeds
10 fresh curry leaves
1 teaspoon garam masala
3 garlic cloves, crushed
1 teaspoon finely grated ginger
2 long green chillies, seeded and chopped
200 g (7 oz/1 bunch) English spinach, shredded

1 Heat 2 teaspoons of the oil in a large saucepan over medium heat. Add the onion and cook, stirring, for 2 minutes. Add the lentils, tomatoes, cayenne pepper and 750 ml (3 cups) cold water and bring to the boil. Reduce the heat to low and simmer for 30 minutes or until the lentils are very soft and starting to break up, adding a little extra water if necessary.

2 Heat the remaining oil in a small saucepan over medium heat. Add the mustard seeds and curry leaves and cook, stirring, for 30 seconds or until the seeds start to pop. Add the garam masala, garlic, ginger and chillies and cook, stirring, for 1 minute.

3 Add the spice mixture and spinach to the lentils and stir to combine. Cook for 1–2 minutes or until the spinach has just wilted. Serve immediately.

tips It is important to serve the dal as soon as the spinach is added, so it stays vibrant and fresh.

The dal is suitable to freeze, without the spinach, in an airtight container for up to 2 months.

dairy free

Soups are a wonderful way to increase your veggie intake and the addition of eggplant adds richness to this delicious chicken soup.

Moroccan chicken soup

Preparation time: 15 minutes
Cooking time: 50 minutes
Serves 4

1 tablespoon extra virgin olive oil

1 (about 400 g/14 oz) eggplant (aubergine), diced

1 large red onion, finely chopped

3 celery stalks, diced

1 large carrot, diced

2 garlic cloves, crushed

1 teaspoon ground cumin

1 teaspoon smoked paprika

½ teaspoon ground cinnamon

½ teaspoon dried red chilli flakes (optional)

400 g (14 oz) skinless chicken thigh fillets, fat trimmed, diced

2 zucchini (courgettes), diced

4 large tomatoes, chopped

750 ml (3 cups) homemade or salt-reduced gluten-free chicken stock

1 Heat half the oil in a large saucepan over high heat. Cook the eggplant, stirring, for 5–6 minutes until browned. Transfer to a heatproof bowl.

2 Heat the remaining oil in the same pan over medium heat. Cook the onion, celery and carrot, stirring, for 6–7 minutes or until softened. Add the garlic and spices and stir for 1 minute or until fragrant. Add the chicken and stir for 3–4 minutes to brown.

3 Add the zucchini and tomatoes and return the eggplant to the pan. Cook, stirring occasionally, for 2 minutes. Add the stock, bring to the boil, then reduce the heat and simmer for 25–30 minutes until thick. Season to taste.

tips You can also add a small handful of quinoa with the stock in step 3 if you wish.

This soup is suitable to freeze in individual airtight containers for up to 1 month.

vegetarian

Tofu is a rich source of complete vegetarian protein: it contains all the essential amino acids and is rich in phytonutrients, which have disease-fighting and anti-inflammatory properties. Finely chopped macadamia nuts enrich and thicken the sauce.

Tofu and vegetable curry with raita

Preparation time: 20 minutes
Cooking time: 30 minutes
Serves 4

1 tablespoon macadamia oil

350 g (12 oz) firm tofu, cut into cubes

1 eggplant (aubergine), cut into large cubes

1 onion, finely chopped

2 long red chillies, seeded and finely chopped

3 garlic cloves, crushed

2 teaspoons grated ginger

1 teaspoon cumin seeds

2 teaspoons ground coriander

1 teaspoon paprika

4 vine-ripened tomatoes, chopped

375 ml (1½ cups) homemade or salt-reduced gluten-free vegetable stock

2 large carrots, sliced into rounds

150 g (5½ oz) green beans, sliced

2 tablespoons macadamia nuts, finely chopped

Raita, to serve (see tip)

Steamed quinoa or brown rice, to serve

1 Heat 1 teaspoon of the oil in a large wok or non-stick frying pan over high heat. Add the tofu and stir-fry for 2–3 minutes or until golden. Remove the tofu, add 2 more teaspoons oil to the wok and stir-fry the eggplant for 2 minutes or until golden. Remove the eggplant.

2 Reduce the heat to medium, add the remaining oil and stir-fry the onion for 3 minutes or until light golden. Add the chilli, garlic, ginger and spices and stir-fry for 1 minute. Add the tomatoes and stock, bring to the boil, reduce the heat, cover and simmer for 5 minutes. Add the carrots, cover and simmer, stirring occasionally, for 10 minutes.

3 Return the tofu and eggplant to the wok with the green beans. Simmer for 2–3 minutes until the beans are just tender. Stir in the macadamias.

4 Serve the curry with raita and steamed quinoa or brown rice.

tip To make your own raita, combine 260 g (1 cup) natural yoghurt, 1 grated Lebanese (short) cucumber, 2 tablespoons chopped mint, 1 crushed garlic clove and a squeeze of lemon juice.

dairy free

This fish curry is not overly spicy, but has a wonderful depth of flavour due to the curry leaves and spices. Any type of firm white fish fillet will work well, or alternatively you could use salmon or trout. I like to serve it with cauliflower rice or steamed quinoa.

Fragrant fish and bean curry

Preparation time: 20 minutes
Cooking time: 25 minutes
Serves 4

2 garlic cloves, chopped
3 cm (1¼ inch) piece ginger, peeled, chopped
2 long fresh green chillies, chopped, plus extra sliced chilli to serve
2 teaspoons macadamia oil
1 red onion, thinly sliced
½ teaspoon ground turmeric
1 teaspoon ground coriander
2 teaspoons brown mustard seeds
10 fresh curry leaves
250 ml (1 cup) reduced-fat coconut milk
125 ml (½ cup) homemade or salt-reduced gluten-free fish or chicken stock
600 g (1 lb 5 oz) firm white fish fillets, cut into chunks (see tip)
200 g (7 oz) green beans, trimmed, halved
Cauliflower rice, to serve (see page 229)

1 Using a mortar and pestle, pound the garlic, ginger and chilli to make a curry paste. Alternatively, use a small food processor and process until finely chopped.

2 Heat the oil in a large heavy-based saucepan over medium heat. Add the onion and cook, stirring, for 3–4 minutes or until softened. Add the curry paste, dry spices and curry leaves and cook, stirring, for 3–4 minutes or until fragrant. Add the coconut milk and stock and bring to the boil. Reduce the heat and simmer, partially covered, for 10 minutes or until slightly reduced.

3 Add the fish and beans and simmer, covered, for 5 minutes or until the fish is cooked through and the beans are tender. Serve with cauliflower rice, garnished with extra green chilli.

tip Firm white fish fillets such as snapper, ling, barramundi or blue-eye trevalla work well for this recipe.

dairy free

This curry is super easy and relatively quick to make. Make sure you trim the chicken well as thighs do contain more saturated fat than breast, but work so much better in a curry. Macadamia oil is ideal for curries and stir-fries, and is rich in omega-9 fatty acids with anti-inflammatory properties.

Thai yellow chicken curry

Preparation time: 15 minutes
Cooking time: 35 minutes
Serves 4

1 teaspoon macadamia oil

1 red onion, thinly sliced

600 g (1 lb 5 oz) skinless chicken thigh fillets, fat trimmed, cut into 3 cm (1¼ inch) pieces

2 tablespoons gluten-free Thai yellow curry paste

1 lemongrass stem, cut into 4 cm (1½ inch) lengths, bruised

4-5 kaffir lime leaves

250 ml (1 cup) homemade or salt-reduced gluten-free chicken stock

250 ml (1 cup) reduced-fat coconut milk

3 carrots, cut into thick rounds

1 bunch broccolini, cut into 4 cm (1½ inch) lengths

200 g (7 oz) cherry tomatoes, halved

2 teaspoons lime juice

1 teaspoon fish sauce

1 teaspoon coconut sugar

Steamed quinoa, brown rice or cauliflower rice (see page 229), to serve

1 Heat the oil in a large wok or saucepan over medium–high heat. Cook the onion, stirring, for 3–4 minutes or until golden. Add the chicken, curry paste, lemongrass and kaffir lime and cook, stirring, for 5–6 minutes or until fragrant.

2 Add the stock, coconut milk and carrot and bring to the boil. Reduce the heat and simmer, partially covered, for 20 minutes or until the carrot is tender. Add the broccolini and tomatoes and simmer for 5 minutes or until the broccolini is tender. Stir through the lime juice, fish sauce and coconut sugar to taste. Serve with steamed quinoa, brown rice or cauliflower rice.

Legumes are a great addition to curries and stews. They reduce the amount of red meat needed in this curry and therefore lower the saturated fat content. The cost of the meal is also reduced – perfect for families.

Masala beef and red kidney bean curry

Preparation time: 20 minutes (plus overnight soaking)
Cooking time: 1 hour 45 minutes
Serves 4

1½ tablespoons extra virgin olive oil

400 g (14 oz) chuck (blade) steak, trimmed and cut into 2 cm (¾ inch) cubes

1 cinnamon stick

2 fresh bay leaves

2 onions, thinly sliced

90 g (⅓ cup) gluten-free tikka masala curry paste

400 g (14 oz) can diced tomatoes

190 g (1 cup) dried red kidney beans, soaked in cold water overnight

130 g (½ cup) natural yoghurt

Fresh coriander (cilantro) leaves, to garnish (optional)

Lime cheeks, to garnish

Steamed greens, such as broccolini, to serve

1 Preheat the oven to 160°C (325°F). Heat 2 teaspoons of the oil in a large flameproof casserole dish over high heat. Add half the beef and cook, turning, for 2–3 minutes or until golden. Remove from the dish and set aside. Repeat with another 2 teaspoons of the oil and the remaining beef.

2 Return the dish to medium heat. Add the remaining oil, the cinnamon stick and bay leaves and cook, stirring, for 1 minute or until fragrant. Add the onion and cook, stirring occasionally, for 5 minutes or until golden. Add the curry paste and cook, stirring, for 1 minute or until fragrant.

3 Return the beef to the pan. Add the tomatoes, kidney beans and 500 ml (2 cups) water and bring to the boil. Cover, transfer to the oven and bake for 1½ hours or until the beef and beans are very tender. Stir in the yoghurt and serve garnished with coriander leaves (if desired) and lime cheeks, accompanied by steamed greens.

tip The curry, before the yoghurt is added, is suitable to freeze. Put it in airtight containers and cool completely. Cover and freeze for up to 2 months.

poultry

dairy free

Turkey breast is protein-rich and extremely lean: it contains less saturated fat than beef, pork or chicken. Serve this dish with a simple side salad, such as sliced cucumber and vine-ripened tomato.

Turkey larb in cos lettuce cups

Preparation time: 20 minutes
Cooking time: 15 minutes
Serves 4

2 teaspoons macadamia oil
1 tablespoon brown rice
400 g (14 oz) minced (ground) turkey breast (see tip)
1 lemongrass stem, white part only, finely chopped
1 long red chilli, seeded and finely chopped
2 garlic cloves, crushed
1 tablespoon chopped coriander (cilantro) root
2 teaspoons finely grated ginger
200 g (7 oz) green beans, thinly sliced
1 tablespoon lime juice
1 tablespoon fish sauce
2 teaspoons coconut sugar
½ cup mint leaves
½ cup coriander (cilantro) leaves
½ small red onion, thinly sliced
175 g (1½ cups) bean sprouts, trimmed
8 cos (romaine) lettuce leaves

1 Heat 1 teaspoon of the oil in a large wok or non-stick frying pan and stir-fry the rice for 1 minute or until golden brown and aromatic. Cool, then finely crush using a mortar and pestle.

2 Add the remaining oil to the wok over high heat. Add the turkey and stir-fry, breaking up the meat, for 7 minutes or until browned. Add the lemongrass, chilli, garlic, coriander root and ginger and stir-fry for 1 minute or until aromatic. Add the green beans and stir-fry for 2 minutes or until almost tender.

3 Stir in the lime juice, fish sauce and coconut sugar. Remove from the heat and cool slightly then stir in the ground rice, herbs, onion and bean sprouts. Spoon into lettuce cups to serve.

tip Minced pork or chicken work well in place of turkey.

Quinoa flakes are a fantastic gluten-free alternative for crumbing meat, chicken, fish, fishcakes or patties. They stick easily, become crisp and golden once pan-fried, and have more flavour than breadcrumbs.

Parmesan and herb chicken schnitzels with tomato salsa

Preparation time: 20 minutes
Cooking time: 15 minutes
Serves 4

110 g (1 cup) quinoa flakes
35 g (1/3 cup) grated parmesan cheese
2 tablespoons finely snipped chives
2 tablespoons finely chopped parsley
1 teaspoon finely grated lemon zest
35 g (1/4 cup) rice flour
2 eggs, lightly whisked
60 ml (1/4 cup) reduced-fat milk
500 g (1 lb 2 oz) chicken tenderloins
2 tablespoons extra virgin olive oil, approximately
Salad leaves or steamed greens, to serve

TOMATO SALSA

3 ripe roma (plum) tomatoes, diced
1/2 teaspoon dried red chilli flakes
2 teaspoons red wine vinegar
1 1/2 tablespoons extra virgin olive oil

1 Combine the quinoa flakes, parmesan, herbs and lemon zest in a shallow bowl. Put the flour in a second shallow bowl and season with salt and pepper. Put the combined eggs and milk in a third bowl.

2 Dust a chicken tenderloin in the seasoned flour, then dip in the egg mixture and finally press into the quinoa mixture until it is evenly coated. Place on a tray and repeat to coat the remaining tenderloins.

3 To make the tomato salsa, put all the ingredients in a bowl and stir to combine. Season with a pinch of sea salt and freshly ground black pepper, to taste. Set aside.

4 Heat the oil in a large non-stick frying pan over medium–high heat. Cook the crumbed chicken, in batches, for 3 minutes each side or until golden and cooked through, adding a little more oil to the pan as necessary.

5 Serve the chicken schnitzels with the tomato salsa and salad leaves or steamed greens.

dairy free

Chickpeas make a delicious, speedy, low-GI and high-fibre alternative to mashed potatoes. Prepared in this way they have a nutty taste and a creamy texture.

Piri piri chicken with smashed chickpeas

Preparation time: 20 minutes (plus 30 minutes marinating)
Cooking time: 15 minutes
Serves 4

2 large skinless chicken breast fillets (about 250 g/9 oz each)
1 tablespoon extra virgin olive oil
Finely grated zest and juice of 1 lemon
1 teaspoon finely grated lime zest
2 garlic cloves, crushed
½ teaspoon dried chilli flakes
½ teaspoon ground turmeric
Rocket (arugula) leaves, to serve

SMASHED CHICKPEAS

2 teaspoons extra virgin olive oil
1 small red onion, finely chopped
2 garlic cloves, crushed
1 teaspoon ground cumin
1 teaspoon sweet paprika
2 x 400 g (14 oz) cans chickpeas, drained and rinsed (see tip)
125 ml (½ cup) homemade or salt-reduced gluten-free chicken stock
1 tablespoon lemon juice, or to taste

1 Cut each chicken breast horizontally through the middle to give 4 thin fillets. Combine the olive oil, lemon zest and juice, lime zest, garlic, chilli flakes and turmeric in a shallow glass or ceramic dish. Add the chicken and turn to coat. Cover and refrigerate for 30 minutes to marinate.

2 Meanwhile, to make the smashed chickpeas, heat the olive oil in a saucepan over medium heat. Add the onion and cook, stirring, for 5 minutes or until softened. Add the garlic, cumin and paprika and cook, stirring, for 1 minute or until fragrant. Add the chickpeas and stock. Simmer for 2–3 minutes. Transfer the chickpea mixture to a food processor and process until smooth. Add lemon juice to taste and season with sea salt and freshly ground black pepper. Return to a clean saucepan and keep warm.

3 Preheat a chargrill pan or barbecue plate over high heat. Drain excess marinade from the chicken. Grill the chicken for 3 minutes each side, or until lightly charred and cooked through. Slice thickly. Serve with the smashed chickpeas and rocket.

tip You can replace the canned chickpeas with 450 g (2⅔ cups) cooked chickpeas.

dairy free

Cauliflower makes a fantastic substitute for rice in this take on traditional fried rice. Low in carbohydrates, providing an extra serve of vegetables, packed with cancer-fighting antioxidants and full of flavour, it is a winner on all levels.

Chicken and cauliflower fried 'rice'

Preparation time: 20 minutes
Cooking time: 15 minutes
Serves 4

1 small head cauliflower (about 750 g/1 lb 10 oz), trimmed and cut into florets

1 tablespoon macadamia oil

250 g (9 oz) skinless chicken breast fillets, thinly sliced

250 g (9 oz) peeled raw prawns (shrimp), tails intact, deveined

1 onion, finely chopped

1 carrot, peeled and cut into thin matchsticks

2 garlic cloves, crushed

2 teaspoons finely grated ginger

200 g (7 oz) snow peas (mangetout), trimmed and sliced

140 g (1 cup) podded fresh or frozen green peas

2 tablespoons gluten-free salt-reduced soy sauce

2 teaspoons gluten-free hot chilli sauce, plus extra to serve

2 tablespoons coarsely chopped coriander (cilantro)

Lime halves, to serve

1 Process the cauliflower in batches in a food processor until it is about the size of rice grains. Don't over-process it; aim to retain some texture. Set aside.

2 Heat half the oil in a large wok over high heat. Stir-fry the chicken and prawns in batches for 2 minutes or until golden. Remove from the wok and set aside.

3 Return the wok to high heat, add the remaining oil, the onion and the carrot and stir-fry for 2 minutes or until golden. Add the garlic and ginger and stir-fry for 30 seconds or until fragrant. Add the cauliflower and stir-fry for 2–3 minutes or until tender. Add the snow peas and peas and stir-fry for a further 1–2 minutes or until just tender.

4 Return the chicken and prawns to the wok. Add the soy sauce and chilli sauce and stir-fry until heated through. Remove from the heat and stir in the coriander. Serve with hot chilli sauce and lime halves.

dairy free

Chicken breasts these days tend to be very large, too much for one serving. I like to slice them through the middle to give two thin fillets per breast. This means they take only a few minutes to cook on each side and they don't dry out or become tough.

Grilled maple and mustard chicken with fennel and asparagus salad

Preparation time: 15 minutes
(plus 30 minutes marinating)
Cooking time: 10 minutes
Serves 4

- 2 x 250 g (9 oz) skinless chicken breast fillets
- 1 tablespoon dijon mustard (see tip)
- 1 tablespoon pure maple syrup
- Finely grated zest and juice of 1 lime
- 1 tablespoon extra virgin olive oil
- Extra virgin olive oil spray
- 2 fennel bulbs, cut into 5 mm ($^1/_4$ inch) thick slices
- 2 bunches asparagus (about 16 spears)
- 200 g (7 oz) grape tomatoes, halved
- 100 g ($3^1/_2$ oz) rocket (arugula) leaves
- 2 teaspoons balsamic vinegar

1 Cut each chicken breast through the middle horizontally to give 4 thin fillets. Combine the mustard, maple syrup, lime zest, lime juice and 2 teaspoons of the olive oil in a shallow glass or ceramic dish. Add the chicken and turn to coat. Cover and set aside in the refrigerator to marinate for at least 30 minutes.

2 Preheat a chargrill pan or barbecue to medium–high. Drain the excess marinade from the chicken and grill the chicken for 2–3 minutes each side or until lightly charred and cooked through. Transfer to a plate and keep warm. Spray the fennel and asparagus with olive oil and grill for 1–2 minutes each side or until just tender.

3 Combine the fennel, asparagus, tomatoes and rocket in a large bowl. Add the remaining olive oil and the vinegar and toss to combine. Serve the chicken with the fennel and asparagus salad.

tip Dijon mustard should be gluten-free, but always check the label.

dairy free

Poaching is a wonderful way to cook chicken breast. It's fat-free and keeps the chicken deliciously moist and tender.

Poached chicken, broad bean and apple salad with toasted seeds

Preparation time: 20 minutes
Cooking time: 40 minutes
Serves 4

- 1 onion, halved
- 1 tablespoon black peppercorns
- 500 g (1 lb 2 oz) skinless chicken breast fillets
- 400 g (14 oz) podded fresh or frozen broad (fava) beans
- 100 g (2¼ cups, firmly packed) English spinach leaves or baby rocket (arugula)
- 1 red apple, cored and diced (see tip)
- 2 tablespoons lightly toasted sunflower seeds
- 2 tablespoons lightly toasted pepitas (pumpkin seeds)
- 2 tablespoons natural almonds, coarsely chopped
- 2 tablespoons coarsely chopped mint
- 1 tablespoon coarsely chopped dill
- 1 tablespoon walnut oil
- 1 tablespoon white balsamic vinegar
- 2 tablespoons apple juice

1 Put the onion, peppercorns and a pinch of sea salt in a large saucepan with 1.25 litres (5 cups) cold water and bring to the boil. Add the chicken breasts, reduce the heat to low and simmer gently for 5 minutes. Remove from the heat, cover and set aside to continue poaching for 30 minutes. Remove the chicken from the poaching liquid (discard the liquid) and set aside to cool. Coarsely chop the chicken.

2 Meanwhile, cook the broad beans in a large saucepan of boiling water for 3 minutes. Refresh under cold running water. Drain. Peel off the skins and discard.

3 Put the chicken, broad beans, rocket leaves, apple, seeds, almonds and herbs in a large bowl. Whisk together the walnut oil, vinegar and apple juice. Add to the salad and gently toss to combine. Serve immediately.

tip To prevent the apple from discolouring, squeeze a little lemon juice over it.

Lean turkey (without skin) is extremely lean, being lower in saturated fat than red meat or chicken, and yet packed with protein. To up the veggie content, serve the meatballs on vegetable 'zoodles' – zucchini, carrot or sweet potato all work well.

Baked turkey meatballs

Preparation time: 20 minutes
Cooking time: 40 minutes
Serves 4

Extra virgin olive oil spray

500 g (1 lb 2 oz) minced (ground) turkey breast

2 tablespoons chopped fresh oregano

2 tablespoons chopped fresh basil

1 small carrot, peeled, finely grated

2 tablespoons finely grated parmesan cheese

2 teaspoons finely grated lemon zest

1 tablespoon extra virgin olive oil

1 onion, finely chopped

2 garlic cloves, crushed

1 zucchini (courgette), diced

1 tablespoon no-added-salt tomato paste (concentrated purée)

400 g (14 oz) can diced tomatoes

Steamed vegetable zoodles, to serve (see tips)

1 Preheat the oven to 180°C (350°F). Lightly spray a 1.5 litre (6 cup) ovenproof dish with oil.

2 Combine the turkey mince, oregano, basil, carrot, parmesan and lemon zest in a large bowl. Season well with salt and pepper. Shape the mixture into 16 meatballs.

3 Heat half the oil in a large non-stick frying pan over medium–high heat. Cook the meatballs, turning, for 3–4 minutes or until golden. Transfer to the ovenproof dish.

4 Heat remaining oil in the same pan and heat over medium heat. Cook the onion, stirring, for 5 minutes or until softened. Add the garlic and zucchini and cook, stirring for 1 minute or until fragrant. Stir in the tomato paste then add the tomatoes and 125 ml (½ cup) water and bring to the boil. Reduce the heat and simmer for 10 minutes or until sauce is thick. Carefully pour the tomato mixture over the meatballs and bake for 20–25 minutes.

5 Serve the meatballs on vegetable zoodles.

---

tips Vegetable 'zoodles' can be made using a spiraliser or vegetable peeler, or can be bought from most major supermarkets.

Meatballs are suitable to freeze (without zoodles). Place in airtight containers, cover and freeze for up to 1 month.

dairy free

Spices such as ginger and cinnamon not only contain powerful compounds with proven anti-inflammatory properties, they are a wonderful way of boosting flavour without added fat, sodium or sugar.

Chicken, sweet potato and date tagine with preserved lemon

Preparation time: 20 minutes
Cooking time: 40 minutes
Serves 4

2 teaspoons extra virgin olive oil
600 g (1 lb 5 oz) skinless chicken thigh fillets, fat trimmed, cut into 2 cm (3/4 inch) cubes
1 large red onion, thinly sliced
2 garlic cloves, crushed
2 teaspoons finely grated fresh ginger
1½ teaspoons ground cumin
1 teaspoon ground coriander
1 cinnamon stick
375 ml (1½ cups) homemade or salt-reduced gluten-free chicken stock
3 fresh dates, pitted, chopped
500 g (1 lb 2 oz) sweet potato, peeled, cut into cubes
150 g (5½ oz) green beans, sliced
1 preserved lemon quarter, white pith removed, rinsed, finely chopped
Coriander (cilantro) leaves, to garnish
Toasted flaked almonds, to garnish

1 Heat half the olive oil in a large heavy-based saucepan over medium–high heat. Cook the chicken, stirring, in 2 batches, for 2–3 minutes or until browned. Transfer to a heatproof bowl.

2 Heat the remaining oil in the same pan over medium heat. Cook the onion, stirring, for 5 minutes or until soft. Add the garlic, ginger and dry spices and cook, stirring, for 1–2 minutes or until fragrant

3 Return the chicken to the pan with the stock, dates and sweet potato and bring to the boil. Reduce the heat and simmer, covered, for 15–20 minutes or until the sweet potato is tender. Add the beans and simmer, uncovered, for 5 minutes or until tender and slightly reduced.

4 Serve the tagine topped with the preserved lemon and garnished with coriander leaves and toasted almonds.

tip This tagine is suitable to freeze before the coriander and almonds are added. Place in individual airtight containers, cool, then cover and freeze for up to 1 month.

dairy free

Nothing beats a homemade roast chicken, stuffed with brown rice, kale and harissa. The skin is high in saturated fat, so you may wish to remove it before eating; the flavour will still be amazing. Serve with loads of steamed green veggies.

Spice-rubbed roast chicken stuffed with harissa, kale and rice

Preparation time: 25 minutes
Cooking time: 1 hour 20 minutes
Serves 4–6

1 tablespoon extra virgin olive oil

1 red onion, finely chopped

2 garlic cloves, crushed

2 teaspoons harissa (see tip)

100 g (3½ oz) kale, chopped

170 g (1 cup) cooked brown rice

1 preserved lemon quarter, rinsed, flesh and pith removed, zest finely chopped

2 tablespoons chopped flat-leaf (Italian) parsley

1 teaspoon cumin seeds

1 teaspoon coriander seeds

¼ teaspoon ground cinnamon

1.6 kg (3 lb 8 oz) free-range chicken, cavity rinsed and patted dry

Steamed green vegetables, to serve

1 Heat 2 teaspoons of the oil in a large non-stick frying pan over medium heat. Add the onion and cook, stirring, for 5 minutes or until softened. Add the garlic and harissa and cook, stirring, for 30 seconds or until aromatic. Add the kale and cook, stirring, for 1–2 minutes or until wilted. Stir in the rice, preserved lemon and parsley. Remove from the heat and cool completely.

2 Stir the cumin and coriander seeds in a small frying pan over low heat for 2 minutes. Transfer to a mortar, cool, then add the cinnamon and a large pinch of salt and, using the pestle, pound until finely ground.

3 Preheat the oven to 220°C (425°F). Spoon the rice mixture into the chicken cavity. Tie the legs together with kitchen string and put the chicken, breast side up, in a large roasting dish. Rub with the remaining oil, then sprinkle with the spice mixture and rub into the chicken skin.

4 Roast the chicken for 20 minutes, then reduce the oven to 190°C (375°F) and cook for 50 minutes or until the juices run clear when you pierce the thigh with a skewer. (If the chicken browns too quickly, cover with foil.) Remove from the oven and cover with foil, and let rest for 10 minutes before carving. Serve with the steamed green vegetables.

tip Harissa should be gluten-free, but always check the label.

dairy free

Filled with shredded vegetables, minced lean chicken and protein-packed eggs, this version of a Japanese pancake makes a nutritious and filling lunch or light dinner. In Japan it's traditionally served with mayonnaise, but I skip this in favour of a little sweet soy sauce and some salad leaves.

Japanese pancakes with mushrooms and chicken

Preparation time: 20 minutes (plus cooling time)
Cooking time: 35 minutes
Makes 8

75 g (1/2 cup) gluten-free or wholemeal plain (all-purpose) flour

3 eggs

1½ tablespoons macadamia oil

200 g (7 oz) minced (ground) chicken or pork

150 g (5½ oz) mushrooms, finely chopped

2 teaspoons finely grated ginger

1 garlic clove, crushed

130 g (1¾ cups) shredded savoy cabbage

1 large carrot, coarsely grated

Gluten-free sweet soy sauce, for drizzling

2 teaspoons sesame seeds, lightly toasted

Sliced spring onions (scallions), to serve

Baby kale leaves, to serve

1 Whisk together the flour, eggs and 80 ml (1/3 cup) cold water until smooth. Season with sea salt and freshly ground black pepper. Set aside.

2 Heat 2 teaspoons of the oil in a large non-stick frying pan. Add the chicken and cook, breaking it up with a wooden spoon, for 5 minutes or until browned. Add the mushrooms, ginger and garlic and cook, stirring, for 3 minutes or until golden. Leave to cool completely.

3 Stir the chicken mixture, cabbage and carrot into the egg batter.

4 Heat half the remaining oil in a large non-stick frying pan over medium–high heat. Ladle ½ cup of batter per pancake into the pan and spread it out to 1 cm (½ inch) thick. Cook for 3 minutes each side or until golden. Transfer to a plate and keep warm while you cook the rest, adding a little more oil when necessary.

5 Serve the pancakes drizzled with a little sweet soy sauce and scattered with the sesame seeds, spring onions and kale leaves.

dairy free

Tray bakes are the perfect quick and easy family meal. Cooking the chicken on the vegetables keeps the chicken deliciously moist, so it's a great way to cook super-lean chicken breast. You can use pretty much any combination of veggies you have on hand.

Spiced chicken tray bake

Preparation time: 10 minutes (plus one hour marinating)
Cooking time: 25–30 minutes
Serves 4

2 tablespoons orange juice
1 teaspoon ground cumin
1 teaspoon ground paprika
½ teaspoon dried chilli flakes
1 tablespoon chopped fresh rosemary
2 teaspoons extra virgin olive oil
4 x 150 g (5½ oz) skinless chicken breast fillets
1 bunch baby carrots, trimmed, scrubbed
Extra virgin olive oil spray
175 g (6 oz) baby capsicums (peppers), halved, seeded (see tip)
2 bunches asparagus, trimmed

1 Combine the orange juice, spices, rosemary and oil in a shallow dish. Season with salt and pepper. Add the chicken and turn to coat. Place in fridge for 1 hour.

2 Preheat the oven to 200°C (400°F). Line a baking tray with baking paper. Place the carrots on the tray and lightly spray with oil. Bake for 10 minutes. Add the chicken and capsicums and lightly spray with a little more oil. Bake for 10 minutes. Add the asparagus and bake for a further 5–10 minutes or until the chicken is cooked through and the vegetables are golden and tender.

tip Baby capsicums can be replaced with 1 red and 1 yellow capsicum, cut into wedges.

dairy free

This salad is equally delicious with or without the chicken. Even as a vegetarian dish, it provides a complete protein, thanks to the combination of quinoa and black beans.

Quinoa, black bean, chicken, sweetcorn and pea salad

Preparation time: 15 minutes
Cooking time: 30 minutes
Serves 4

200 g (1 cup) quinoa, rinsed and drained (see tips)

140 g (1 cup) fresh or frozen green peas

400 g (14 oz) skinless chicken breast fillets (about 2 fillets)

1 sweetcorn cob

400 g (14 oz) can black beans, drained and rinsed (see tips)

¼ cup mint leaves, coarsely chopped, plus extra whole leaves to garnish

1½ tablespoons lime juice

1½ tablespoons extra virgin olive oil

1 teaspoon single origin floral honey

Pinch of dried chilli flakes

1 Put the quinoa in a large saucepan with 435 ml (1¾ cups) cold water. Bring to the boil, reduce heat to low, cover and simmer until all the water has been absorbed, about 12–15 minutes. Transfer to a bowl and set aside for 10 minutes.

2 Meanwhile, cook the peas in a saucepan of boiling water until just tender. Refresh under cold running water. Drain well and add to the bowl with the quinoa.

3 Cut each chicken breast horizontally through the middle to give 4 thin fillets. Heat a large chargrill pan or non-stick frying pan over high heat. Add the corn and cook, turning, for 6–8 minutes or until lightly charred. Remove the corn from the pan and set aside. Add the chicken and cook for 2–3 minutes each side or until golden and cooked through. Set the chicken and corn aside to cool slightly. Cut the kernels from the corn and thinly slice the chicken. Add the corn, chicken, black beans and chopped mint to the quinoa mixture.

4 Whisk the lime juice, olive oil, honey and chilli flakes together in a small bowl. Add to the quinoa mixture, season to taste with sea salt and freshly ground black pepper and gently toss to combine. Garnish with extra mint leaves and serve.

tips Quinoa has a natural coating of bitter-tasting saponins and most quinoa is sold pre-rinsed. It's important, however, to rinse quinoa until the water runs clear to remove any residual bitterness.

You can replace the canned black beans with 255 g (1½ cups) cooked black beans, or red kidney beans or pinto beans.

dairy free

This salad is fresh, light and full of flavour. The peanuts add a delicious crunch, plus a good dose of anti-inflammatory monounsaturated fatty acids and vitamin E. To make a more substantial meal, add half a cup of steamed wholegrain brown rice or quinoa per person.

Spicy chicken salad with peanuts, cabbage and mint

Preparation time: 20 minutes
Cooking time: 5 minutes
Serves 4

½ small red cabbage (about 800 g/ 1 lb 12 oz), trimmed and shredded

200 g (7 oz) cherry tomatoes, halved

½ cup mint leaves

½ cup coriander (cilantro) leaves

50 g (⅓ cup) unsalted roasted peanuts, coarsely chopped

400 g (14 oz) minced (ground) chicken (see tips)

1 lemongrass stem, pale part only, finely chopped

2 red Asian shallots, finely chopped

2 teaspoons macadamia oil

DRESSING

2 tablespoons lime juice

1 tablespoon fish sauce

3 teaspoons coconut sugar

1–2 long red chillies, or to taste, seeded and finely chopped (see tips)

1 To make the dressing, combine the lime juice, fish sauce, coconut sugar and chilli in a small bowl, stirring to dissolve the sugar. Set aside.

2 Combine the cabbage, tomatoes, mint, coriander and peanuts in a large bowl. Set aside.

3 Combine the chicken, lemongrass, shallots and oil in a medium bowl. Heat a wok over high heat. Add the chicken mixture and stir-fry, breaking up the chicken, for 2–3 minutes or until golden. Add to the vegetables, drizzle with the dressing and gently toss to combine. Serve immediately.

tips You can replace the minced chicken with minced turkey, pork or beef.

If you like things really spicy, replace the long red chillies with 1–2 bird's eye chillies.

seafood

Spiced fish and a crunchy salad of cucumber, tomato and toasted coconut make these tacos not only delicious but healthy too. The avocado adds creaminess and a good dose of monounsaturated fats. Choose a firm white fish such as blue-eye trevalla or ling.

Fish tacos with spiced tomato and toasted coconut salad

Preparation time: 20 minutes
Cooking time: 5 minutes
Serves 4

20 g (1/3 cup) coconut flakes
1 teaspoon smoked paprika
1/2 teaspoon ground coriander
Pinch of cayenne pepper
500 g (1 lb 2 oz) firm white fish fillets, cut into 2 cm (3/4 inch) pieces
1½ tablespoons extra virgin olive oil
3 large vine-ripened tomatoes, chopped
2 Lebanese (short) cucumbers, chopped
1/2 firm ripe avocado, diced
1/4 cup coriander (cilantro) leaves, coarsely chopped
1 long red chilli, seeded and finely chopped
Lime juice, to taste, plus lime wedges to serve
8 gluten-free corn tortillas, warmed
Natural yoghurt, to serve

1 Heat a large non-stick frying pan over low heat and cook the coconut flakes, stirring, for 2 minutes or until just golden. Set aside to cool.

2 Combine the paprika, coriander and cayenne pepper and sprinkle evenly over the fish.

3 Heat 1 tablespoon of the oil in a large non-stick frying pan over medium–high heat and cook the fish, turning, for 2–3 minutes until golden and cooked through.

4 Toss together the coconut, tomato, cucumber, avocado, coriander and chilli in a large bowl. Add the remaining olive oil and lime juice to taste. Season with sea salt and freshly ground black pepper.

5 Serve the fish and salad in the warmed tortillas with a wedge of lime and a dollop of yoghurt.

dairy free

Grilled or barbecued squid is a low-fat, low-kilojoule source of protein, rich in B vitamins. Here it's tossed with a spicy Asian salad to make a delicious light meal.

Chilli squid salad with cucumber, mango and lemongrass

Preparation time: 25 minutes
(plus 30 minutes marinating)
Cooking time: 5 minutes
Serves 4

600 g (1 lb 5 oz) cleaned baby squid
1 lemongrass stem, pale part only, finely chopped
1 long red chilli, seeded and finely chopped
1 tablespoon finely chopped coriander (cilantro) root
1 tablespoon lime juice
2 teaspoons macadamia oil
2 Lebanese (short) cucumbers
1 large firm ripe mango, diced
150 g (5½ oz) sugar snap peas, sliced
⅓ cup mint leaves
⅓ cup coriander (cilantro) leaves
⅓ cup basil leaves
1 Asian shallot, finely chopped
2 tablespoons unsalted roasted peanuts, chopped

CHILLI DRESSING

1½ tablespoons lime juice
2 teaspoons fish sauce
2 teaspoons coconut sugar
1 long red chilli, seeded and finely chopped
1 teaspoon finely grated ginger

1 Cut the squid hoods open and score the insides in a crisscross pattern, then cut each hood into 3 cm (1¼ inch) pieces. Mix the lemongrass, chilli, coriander root, lime juice and oil in a shallow non-metallic dish, add the squid and stir to coat. Cover and refrigerate for 30 minutes.

2 Meanwhile, for the chilli dressing, combine the ingredients in a bowl, stirring to dissolve the coconut sugar.

3 Cut the cucumbers into long thin ribbons with a peeler, stopping when you reach the seeds, and place in a large bowl. Add the mango, sugar snap peas, herbs and shallot.

4 Heat a large chargrill pan or barbecue plate to high heat. Drain the squid and grill for 1–2 minutes each side until lightly charred and just cooked through. Be careful not to overcook or the squid will be tough.

5 Add half the dressing to the salad and toss gently. Serve the salad topped with grilled squid, drizzled with the remaining dressing and sprinkled with peanuts.

dairy free

White fish is an extremely lean source of good-quality protein. In this recipe, it's topped with a simple crust – the macadamias and pepitas add flavour and a good dose of healthy fats and delicious crunch.

Macadamia-crusted fish with garlic greens

Preparation time: 20 minutes
Cooking time: 15 minutes
Serves 4

75 g (½ cup) unsalted raw macadamia nuts (see tip)

¼ cup flat-leaf (Italian) parsley leaves

2 tablespoons pepitas (pumpkin seeds)

2 tablespoons snipped chives

1 garlic clove, crushed, plus 3 extra cloves, thinly sliced

1 teaspoon finely grated lemon zest

1½ tablespoons lemon juice

4 x 125 g (4½ oz) firm white fish fillets

Extra virgin olive oil spray

2 teaspoons extra virgin olive oil

250 g (9 oz) kale, coarsely chopped

¼ green cabbage, coarsely chopped

1 Preheat the oven to 200°C (400°F). Line a large baking tray with baking paper.

2 Finely chop the macadamias, parsley, pepitas and chives in a food processor. Add the crushed garlic, lemon zest and 1 tablespoon of the lemon juice and process to a coarse paste, adding 1–2 teaspoons water if needed.

3 Press the macadamia mixture onto one side of the fish. Place the fish, nut side up, on the tray, spray lightly with olive oil and bake for 12 minutes or until the thickest part of the flesh flakes easily.

4 Meanwhile, heat the oil in a large wok or non-stick frying pan over medium–high heat. Stir-fry the sliced garlic for 30 seconds or until aromatic. Add the kale and cabbage and stir-fry for 2–3 minutes or until just wilted. Add the remaining lemon juice and season to taste.

5 Serve the fish on the garlic greens.

tip You can replace the macadamias with cashews or almonds.

dairy free

Canned sardines are versatile, cost effective and a wonderful source of marine omega-3 fatty acids, which are known to reduce inflammation. They are a little stronger in flavour than other fish, but are the perfect match to fresh basil and roasted tomatoes.

Roasted fennel, potato, tomato and sardine salad

Preparation time: 20 minutes
Cooking time: 35 minutes
Serves 4

750 g (1 lb 10 oz) baby potatoes, halved

2 fennel bulbs, trimmed, cut into thin wedges

Extra virgin olive oil spray

250 g (9 oz) cherry tomatoes, halved

250 g (9 oz) green beans, trimmed, halved

½ cup fresh basil leaves

½ cup fresh flat-leaf (Italian) parsley leaves

40 g (⅓ cup) pitted green olives, sliced

2 tablespoons extra virgin olive oil

1 tablespoon lemon juice

1 teaspoon finely grated lemon zest

3 x 110 g (3¾ oz) cans sardines in extra virgin olive oil, drained

4 poached eggs, to serve

1 Preheat the oven to 200°C (400°F) and line a large baking tray with baking paper.

2 Place the potatoes in a microwave-safe dish. Cover and microwave on high (100%) for 4 minutes. Drain.

3 Place the potatoes and fennel on the baking tray and lightly spray with oil. Bake for 30 minutes or until the vegetables are golden and tender. Add the tomatoes to the tray for the last 10 minutes of cooking time.

4 Meanwhile, cook the beans in a saucepan of boiling water until just tender. Drain.

5 Combine the roasted vegetables, beans, basil, parsley and olives in a large bowl. Season with salt and freshly ground black pepper. Whisk the oil, lemon juice and zest together in a small bowl, add to the salad and gently toss to combine.

6 To serve, divide the salad among 4 bowls. Top each with the sardines and a poached egg.

dairy free

Super-fast and easy, this dish can be made from any type of firm white fish fillets. Serve it with lots of steamed greens – bok choy and asparagus, for example – and if you're extra hungry, add half a cup of steamed brown rice or quinoa per person.

Steamed fish with ginger, spring onions and sesame

Preparation time: 5 minutes
Cooking time: 10 minutes
Serves 4

4 x 125 g (4½ oz) firm white fish fillets (see tip)

3 cm (1¼ inch) piece ginger, cut into matchsticks

4 spring onions (scallions), thinly sliced

100 g (3½ oz) cherry tomatoes, halved

1 tablespoon macadamia oil

1 tablespoon gluten-free salt-reduced soy sauce

2 teaspoons sesame oil

Steamed Asian greens, to serve

1 Line a large steamer with baking paper. Add the fish fillets in a single layer and sprinkle with the ginger and spring onions. Arrange the tomatoes on top. Cover and place over a wok or saucepan of simmering water, ensuring the steamer doesn't touch the water. Steam for 6–8 minutes or until the thickest part of the fish flakes easily.

2 Meanwhile, combine the macadamia oil, soy sauce and sesame oil in a small saucepan and bring to the boil.

3 Transfer the fish to plates and drizzle with the hot oil. Serve immediately with steamed Asian greens.

tip Barramundi and blue-eye trevalla work well in this recipe.

dairy free

Diets rich in omega-3 fatty acids have been linked to a lower risk of cardiovascular disease, as well as having an anti-inflammatory effect. Tuna is a good source of these omega-3s, while the apple salad and ponzu dressing cut through the richness of the fish. This dish is worthy of a dinner party; it's also versatile enough for lunch.

Tuna tataki on smashed avocado with apple salad and ponzu dressing

Preparation time: 25 minutes
Cooking time: 1 minute
Serves 4

1 large avocado, diced

2 teaspoons sesame seeds, lightly toasted, plus extra to garnish

3 spring onions (scallions), thinly sliced

2 teaspoons lemon juice

500 g (1 lb 2 oz) piece tuna loin (see tips)

2 teaspoons macadamia or extra virgin olive oil

75 g (1½ cups) baby English spinach leaves

25 g (1 oz) beetroot (beet) leaves

1 Lebanese (short) cucumber, seeded and cut into matchsticks

1 green apple, cut into matchsticks (see tips)

PONZU DRESSING

2 tablespoons gluten-free salt-reduced soy sauce

1 tablespoon lemon juice

1 tablespoon gluten-free mirin

½ teaspoon finely grated ginger

1 Whisk together the ponzu dressing ingredients and refrigerate.

2 Roughly mash the avocado and mix with the toasted sesame seeds, spring onions and lemon juice. Season to taste.

3 Heat a large chargrill pan or non-stick frying pan over high heat. Brush the tuna with oil and season to taste. Sear the tuna for 20–30 seconds each side. Cool, then cut into slices.

4 Mix together the spinach, beetroot leaves, cucumber and apple.

5 Spread the avocado mixture on plates. Top with the apple salad and tuna slices and drizzle with the ponzu dressing. Garnish with extra toasted sesame seeds.

tips It's important not to overcook the tuna – it should be just seared. Tuna loin can be difficult to obtain. You can replace the loin with four 125 g (4½ oz) tuna steaks.

To prevent the apple discolouring, toss it with a little lemon juice as soon as you cut it.

dairy free

Chia seeds are a great alternative to breadcrumb crusts for those on a gluten-free diet. Chia seeds, the highest plant source of omega-3 fatty acids, and salmon ensure this meal is packed with essential fatty acids.

Chia-crusted salmon with Asian greens and soy dressing

Preparation time: 10 minutes
Cooking time: 10 minutes
Serves 4

2 tablespoons white chia seeds

2 tablespoons black chia seeds

4 x 125 g (4½ oz) skinless salmon fillets

2 bunches choy sum, washed and trimmed

2 tablespoons macadamia oil

3 cm (1¼ inch) piece ginger, peeled and julienned

2 garlic cloves, thinly sliced

Gluten-free or wholegrain noodles, or steamed brown rice, to serve

SOY DRESSING

2 tablespoons gluten-free oyster sauce

2 tablespoons gluten-free salt-reduced soy sauce

1 tablespoon Chinese rice wine (see tip)

1 teaspoon single origin floral honey

1 Combine the white and black chia seeds on a plate. Press each salmon fillet in the chia seeds to evenly coat one side, then set aside.

2 Remove the stems from the choy sum, cut in half if long and reserve. To make the soy dressing, put all the ingredients in a small bowl and stir to combine.

3 Heat 1 tablespoon of the oil in a large non-stick frying pan over high heat. Cook the salmon, chia side down, for 2–3 minutes or until golden. Turn and cook for a further 2 minutes (for medium) or until cooked to your liking. Set aside and keep warm.

4 Meanwhile, heat the remaining oil in a large wok or frying pan over high heat. Add the ginger and garlic and stir-fry for 30 seconds. Add the choy sum stems and stir-fry for 1–2 minutes, then add the choy sum leaves and stir-fry for 1 minute more or until almost wilted. Add half the dressing and toss to combine.

5 To serve, divide the choy sum among serving plates, top each with a piece of salmon and drizzle over a little of the remaining dressing. Serve with noodles or steamed rice.

tip Chinese rice wine should be gluten-free, but always check the label.

dairy free

Trout is loaded with omega-3 essential fatty acids, the natural anti-inflammatory warriors. Combine it with tomato, zucchini and fennel for a super-quick yet delicious dinner that can be on the table in just 20 minutes. Serve with steamed veggies or a big green salad to boost the veggie content.

Barbecued trout parcels with fennel, zucchini and tomato

Preparation time: 10 minutes
Cooking time: 10 minutes
Serves 4

200 g (7 oz) grape tomatoes, quartered

1 tablespoon salted baby capers, rinsed, drained, and chopped

2 teaspoons lemon juice

2 teaspoons extra virgin olive oil

1 medium fennel bulb, trimmed, thinly sliced

2 small zucchini (courgettes), cut into 1 cm (1/2 inch) thick slices

4 x 125 g (4 1/2 oz) skinless ocean trout fillets (see tips)

Lemon wedges, to serve

1 tablespoon chopped fresh chives, to serve

Steamed green vegetables, to serve

1 Combine the tomatoes, capers, lemon juice and oil in a small bowl. Season with salt and freshly ground black pepper.

2 Cut four 30 cm (12 inch) squares of foil and four 30 cm squares of baking paper. Place 1 piece of baking paper on top of each piece of foil. Place the fennel, zucchini and a piece of trout in the centre of the baking paper squares. Spoon over the tomato mixture. Fold the baking paper, then the foil, to form a parcel and enclose the filling.

3 Preheat a hooded barbecue on high heat. Cook the parcels, with hood down, for 10 minutes or until the fish is cooked to your liking (see tips). Serve with lemon wedges, chives and steamed green vegetables.

tips Salmon or any firm white fish fillet such as snapper, barramundi or ling also work well in this recipe.

You can cook the parcels in an oven preheated to 220°C (425°F) for 12–15 minutes instead of the barbecue.

dairy free

Canned salmon is an extremely cost-effective way to include fish in your diet. Oily fish such as salmon are loaded with anti-inflammatory omega-3 fatty acids, plus canned salmon (with small bones) is also an excellent source of calcium.

Salmon, quinoa and dill fish cakes

Preparation time: 15 minutes (plus 30 minutes chilling)
Cooking time: 20 minutes
Serves 4

500 g (1 lb 2 oz) peeled sweet potato, cut into 3 cm (1¼ inch) cubes

150 g (5½ oz) green beans, trimmed

2 celery stalks, finely chopped

415 g (14¾ oz) can pink or red salmon, drained, flaked

2 tablespoons chopped fresh chives

2 tablespoons chopped fresh dill

2 tablespoons gluten-free or wholemeal plain (all-purpose) flour

Finely grated zest of 1 lemon

55 g (½ cup) quinoa flakes

1 tablespoon extra virgin olive oil

Mixed salad leaves and lemon wedges, to serve

1 Steam the sweet potato in a steamer over a saucepan of simmering water for 12 minutes or until tender. Drain. Transfer to a bowl, and mash roughly with a fork. Set aside to cool.

2 Meanwhile, place the beans in a steamer over a saucepan of simmering water. Cover and steam for 4 minutes or until tender. Drain. Refresh under cold running water and drain again. Thinly slice into rounds.

3 Place the cooled mashed sweet potato, beans, celery, salmon, chives, dill, flour and lemon zest in a large bowl. Season with salt and freshly ground black pepper and stir until well combined.

4 Using your hands, divide the mixture into 8 portions and shape into patties. Place the quinoa flakes on a large plate. Press the fish cakes into the flakes to lightly coat. Cover and refrigerate for 30 minutes to firm.

5 Heat the oil in a large non-stick frying pan over medium–high heat. Cook the fish cakes for 2–3 minutes each side or until golden brown. Serve with mixed salad leaves and lemon wedges.

dairy free

This is the perfect summer salad – light, healthy and easy to cook on the barbecue. The cannellini beans make it filling and substantial enough for dinner. Feel free to use white beans of any sort.

Grilled seafood salad with beans, dill and lemon dressing

Preparation time: 20 minutes (plus 1–2 hours marinating)
Cooking time: 15 minutes
Serves 4

2 tablespoons extra virgin olive oil

1 long red chilli, seeded and finely chopped

2 garlic cloves, crushed

500 g (1 lb 2 oz) baby calamari, cleaned, tentacles reserved

300 g (10½ oz) peeled raw prawns (shrimp), deveined, tails intact

2 tablespoons coarsely chopped dill

1½ tablespoons lemon juice

1 teaspoon finely grated lemon zest

400 g (14 oz) can cannellini beans, drained and rinsed (see tip)

16 asparagus spears, trimmed

Extra virgin olive oil spray

100 g (3½ oz) baby rocket (arugula) leaves

Lemon wedges, to garnish

1 Combine 1 tablespoon of the olive oil, the chilli and garlic in a shallow glass or ceramic dish. Score the inside of the calamari bodies and cut into 4 cm (1½ inch) squares. Add them to the olive oil mixture along with the reserved tentacles and prawns and stir to coat. Cover and set aside in the refrigerator to marinate for 1–2 hours.

2 Combine the remaining olive oil, dill, lemon juice and zest in a large bowl. Add the cannellini beans and stir to coat.

3 Preheat a chargrill pan or barbecue plate over high heat. Spray the asparagus lightly with olive oil. Grill the asparagus for 1 minute each side or until lightly charred and tender. Add to the bean mixture.

4 Grill the calamari and prawns in batches for 1–2 minutes each side or until lightly charred and just cooked (be careful not to overcook the calamari or it will become tough). Remove and add to the bean mixture. Add the rocket and gently toss to combine. Serve immediately with lemon wedges.

tip You can replace the canned cannellini beans with 240 g (1⅓ cups) cooked cannellini beans.

dairy free

Whole fish are surprisingly easy to cook. A fresh herb and spice paste, too, takes only minutes to make, and adds a huge amount of flavour. Serve this with lots of steamed Asian greens and some wholegrain brown rice or quinoa to make a balanced meal.

Baked whole snapper with Moroccan spice paste

Preparation time: 15 minutes (plus 30 minutes marinating)
Cooking time: 25 minutes
Serves 4

- ½ cup (firmly packed) coriander (cilantro) leaves, plus extra to garnish
- ½ cup (firmly packed) mint leaves, plus extra to garnish
- 1 long red chilli, seeded and finely chopped
- 1 garlic clove
- 1 teaspoon grated ginger
- 1 teaspoon ground cumin
- 1 lemon, thinly sliced, plus 1 tablespoon lemon juice
- 2 teaspoons extra virgin olive oil
- 1 kg (2 lb 4 oz) whole snapper, scaled and gutted (see tip)
- Steamed Asian greens, to serve

1 Finely chop the herbs, chilli, garlic, ginger and cumin in a food processor. Add the lemon juice, olive oil and 1–2 tablespoons water or enough to form a smooth paste. Process until smooth.

2 Cut three deep diagonal slashes through the skin and down to the bone on each side of the fish. Place the fish in a large non-metallic dish and fill the cavity with the lemon slices. Pour the spice paste over the fish and turn to coat well. Cover and refrigerate for at least 30 minutes.

3 Preheat the oven to 220°C (425°F). Put the fish on a large baking paper-lined baking tray and roast for 20–25 minutes or until the thickest part of the flesh flakes easily. Serve garnished with steamed Asian greens and the extra herbs.

tip You could use 2 baby snapper (500 g/1 lb 2 oz each) in place of the larger one. The cooking time will decrease to 15–20 minutes.

dairy free

Quinoa is a great wholegrain alternative to jasmine rice in Asian stir-fries. Not only do whole grains lower blood levels of C-reactive protein, nutritionally they are superior to white rice – with twice as much protein, significantly more dietary fibre and more of the micronutrients potassium, calcium and magnesium.

Prawn, quinoa and vegetable stir-fry

Preparation time: 20 minutes
(plus 30 minutes marinating)
Cooking time: 25 minutes
Serves 4

- **½ teaspoon chilli flakes**
- **3 garlic cloves, crushed**
- **2 teaspoons finely grated ginger**
- **1½ tablespoons macadamia oil**
- **400 g (14 oz) peeled raw prawns (shrimp), tails intact**
- **150 g (¾ cup) quinoa, rinsed**
- **1 large onion, finely chopped**
- **1 bunch asparagus (about 8 spears), sliced**
- **200 g (7 oz) sugar snap peas, sliced**
- **½ small red cabbage, shredded**
- **2 tablespoons gluten-free salt-reduced soy sauce (see tip)**

1 Combine the chilli flakes, half the garlic, half the ginger and 2 teaspoons of the oil in a shallow non-metallic dish. Add the prawns and turn to coat well. Cover and refrigerate for 30 minutes.

2 Meanwhile, put the quinoa with 375 ml (1½ cups) cold water in a saucepan. Bring to the boil, cover, reduce the heat to low and simmer for 12 minutes or until the water has been absorbed and the quinoa is al dente.

3 Heat 2 teaspoons of the oil in a large wok or non-stick frying pan over high heat. Stir-fry the prawns for 2–3 minutes until golden and just cooked through; remove from the wok.

4 Return the wok to high heat, add the remaining oil and stir-fry the onion for 2–3 minutes. Add the remaining garlic and ginger and stir-fry for 1 minute. Add the asparagus, sugar snaps and 2 tablespoons water and stir-fry for 1–2 minutes.

5 Add the quinoa and cabbage and stir-fry for 1–2 minutes. Add the prawns and soy sauce and toss for 1 minute until heated through.

tip Prawns are quite high in sodium, but using salt-reduced soy sauce keeps the overall sodium content down.

beef, pork & lamb

dairy free

Snake beans, also known as Chinese long beans or yard-long beans, are dark green and crunchy. If you can't find them, use regular green beans.

Ginger beef and bean stir-fry

Preparation time: 15 minutes
Cooking time: 15 minutes
Serves 4

250 g (9 oz) fresh or frozen edamame (soy beans)

1 tablespoon macadamia oil

500 g (1 lb 2 oz) lean rump steak, thinly sliced across the grain

1 white onion, thinly sliced

3 cm (1¼ inch) piece ginger, peeled and cut into thin matchsticks

1 long red chilli, seeded and finely chopped

200 g (7 oz) snake (yard-long) beans, trimmed and sliced

1 red capsicum (pepper), seeded and chopped

2 tablespoons gluten-free oyster sauce

1 tablespoon gluten-free salt-reduced soy sauce

1 tablespoon Chinese rice wine (see tip)

Steamed brown rice, to serve (optional)

Spring onions (scallions), thinly sliced, to garnish (optional)

1 Cook the edamame in a saucepan of boiling water for 1 minute. Refresh under cold running water. Drain. Remove the beans from the pods (discard pods) and set aside.

2 Heat half the oil in a large wok over high heat. Stir-fry the beef in two batches for 2 minutes or until golden. Remove from the wok and set aside.

3 Return the wok to high heat. Add the remaining oil and the onion and stir-fry for 2 minutes. Add the ginger and chilli and stir-fry for 30 seconds or until fragrant. Add the snake beans, capsicum and 2 tablespoons water and stir-fry for 2 minutes or until the vegetables are almost tender-crisp.

4 Return the beef to the wok with the reserved edamame and the oyster sauce, soy sauce and rice wine and stir-fry for 1–2 minutes or until heated through. Serve immediately on steamed brown rice, if desired, garnished with spring onions.

tips Chinese rice wine should be gluten-free, but always check the label.

dairy free

Veal racks are extremely lean, as well as being a good source of iron, protein and B vitamins, which are essential for energy and metabolism. Peas and broad beans, both legumes, are rich in dietary fibre and protein and a low-GI source of carbohydrate.

Herb-crusted veal rack with braised broad beans and peas

Preparation time: 20 minutes
Cooking time: 35 minutes
Serves 4

- ½ cup (lightly packed) flat-leaf (Italian) parsley leaves
- 40 g (1½ oz) gluten-free or wholegrain bread
- 40 g (⅓ cup) walnut halves
- 2 tablespoons chopped sage
- 2 teaspoons dijon mustard (see tips)
- 1 teaspoon single origin floral honey
- 2 tablespoons extra virgin olive oil
- 1 x 4-cutlet French-trimmed veal rack (about 600 g/1 lb 5 oz)
- 2 French shallots, finely chopped
- 2 garlic cloves, crushed
- 350 g (2 cups) podded fresh or frozen broad (fava) beans (see tip)
- 280 g (2 cups) podded fresh or frozen baby green peas (see tips)
- 80 ml (⅓ cup) homemade or salt-reduced gluten-free chicken stock
- 100 g (3½ oz) trimmed silverbeet (Swiss chard), kale or English spinach, chopped

1 Preheat the oven to 200°C (400°F). Process the parsley, bread, walnuts and sage in a food processor until finely chopped. Add the mustard, honey and 1 tablespoon of the oil and pulse until well combined. Press the herb mixture evenly over the top of the veal rack.

2 Place the veal on a roasting rack over a baking tray and drizzle with 2 teaspoons of the oil. Roast to your liking (30–35 minutes, or an internal temperature of 65–70°C/150–160°F, for medium). Transfer to a large plate, cover loosely with foil and rest for 10 minutes.

3 Meanwhile, heat the remaining oil in a large non-stick frying pan over medium heat. Add the shallots and cook, stirring, for 5 minutes or until softened. Add the garlic and cook, stirring, for 30 seconds. Add the broad beans, peas and stock and simmer for 2 minutes. Add the silverbeet and cook, stirring, for 1–2 minutes or until just wilted. Season with sea salt and freshly ground black pepper.

4 Carve the veal into cutlets and serve with the broad beans and peas.

tips Dijon mustard should be gluten-free, but always check the label.

When broad beans and peas are out of season, frozen ones will work perfectly well here.

vegetarian (see tips)

Replacing half the usual amount of meat in a bolognese sauce with lentils is a great way to increase the vegetable content and reduce the total fat and saturated fat content.

Bolognese

Preparation time: 15 minutes
Cooking time: 40 minutes
Serves 4

- **1 tablespoon extra virgin olive oil**
- **1 onion, finely chopped**
- **1 small carrot, peeled and finely chopped**
- **1 celery stalk, finely chopped**
- **1 small zucchini (courgette), trimmed and finely chopped**
- **2 garlic cloves, crushed**
- **2 teaspoons finely chopped rosemary**
- **250 g (9 oz) minced (ground) pork**
- **2 tablespoons no-added-salt tomato paste (concentrated purée)**
- **125 ml (1/2 cup) white wine**
- **400 g (14 oz) can diced tomatoes**
- **400 g (14 oz) can brown lentils, drained and rinsed (see tips)**
- **250 g (9 oz) gluten-free (such as buckwheat) or wholegrain pasta**
- **Freshly grated parmesan cheese, to serve**

1 Heat the olive oil in a large saucepan over medium heat. Add the onion, carrot and celery and cook, stirring, for 6–7 minutes or until softened. Add the zucchini, garlic and rosemary and cook, stirring, for 1 minute. Add the pork and cook, breaking up the meat with a wooden spoon, for 4–5 minutes or until browned.

2 Add the tomato paste and cook, stirring, for 1 minute. Add the wine and simmer until reduced by half. Add the tomatoes and 80 ml (1/3 cup) water and bring to the boil. Reduce the heat to low and simmer for 10 minutes. Add the lentils and simmer for 10 minutes or until thick. Season to taste with sea salt and freshly ground black pepper.

3 Meanwhile, cook the pasta in a large saucepan of lightly salted boiling water according to the packet instructions or until al dente. Drain well, add to the pan with the sauce and toss until well combined. Divide the pasta among bowls and serve with parmesan.

tips For a vegetarian version, omit the pork and double the quantity of lentils.

You can replace the canned lentils with 255 g (1½ cups) cooked brown lentils.

This bolognese is suitable to freeze. Put it in airtight containers, cool completely, cover and freeze for up to 2 months.

dairy free

Snow peas, like all peas, are one of the best vegetable sources of dietary fibre. They are also packed with vitamin C, vitamin B3 (niacin), folate and potassium.

Honey-glazed pork with snow pea, cabbage and sprout slaw

Preparation time: 15 minutes
Cooking time: 20 minutes
Serves 4

60 ml (1/4 cup) orange juice

2 tablespoons single origin floral honey

2 tablespoons gluten-free mirin

1½ tablespoons gluten-free salt-reduced soy sauce

1 teaspoon finely grated ginger

1 teaspoon extra virgin olive oil

500 g (1 lb 2 oz) pork fillets

200 g (7 oz) snow peas (mangetout), trimmed and thinly sliced

1/4 small red cabbage (about 400 g/14 oz), trimmed and shredded

30 g (1 oz) snow pea (mangetout) sprouts, trimmed

2 teaspoons lightly toasted sesame seeds

1 teaspoon macadamia oil

Thinly sliced spring onions (scallions), to garnish

1 Preheat the oven to 200°C (400°F). Combine the orange juice, honey, mirin, 1 tablespoon of the soy sauce and the ginger in a small saucepan. Simmer over medium heat for 3–4 minutes or until syrupy and reduced by half. Set aside.

2 Place a wire rack over a baking tray lined with baking paper. Heat the oil in a large non-stick frying pan over high heat. Cook the pork for 1–2 minutes each side or until browned. Transfer the pork to the rack and brush with half the reserved glaze. Roast for 10 minutes for medium, or until cooked to your liking. Remove, cover loosely with foil and set aside to rest for 3 minutes.

3 Place the snow peas, cabbage, snow pea sprouts, sesame seeds, macadamia oil and remaining 2 teaspoons soy sauce in a large bowl and toss to combine.

4 To serve, thickly slice the pork. Divide the salad and pork among serving plates, drizzle the pork with a little of the remaining glaze, and garnish with the spring onions.

tip It is essential to line the baking tray with baking paper, to prevent the glaze from burning on the bottom of the tray.

dairy free

This stew also makes a delicious vegetarian meal. Simply omit the lamb and serve it with gluten-free or wholegrain flatbread and salad leaves.

Chickpea stew with rosemary and lemon grilled lamb

Preparation time: 20 minutes (plus 30 minutes marinating)
Cooking time: 25 minutes
Serves 4

1 tablespoon extra virgin olive oil
1 tablespoon lemon juice
2 teaspoons rosemary, coarsely chopped
1 teaspoon finely grated lemon zest
12 French-trimmed lamb cutlets
Baby English spinach leaves, to serve

CHICKPEA STEW

2 teaspoons extra virgin olive oil
1 red onion, finely chopped
2 celery stalks, trimmed and diced
2 garlic cloves, crushed
1 teaspoon sweet paprika
1 tablespoon no-added-salt tomato paste (concentrated purée)
2 x 400 g (14 oz) cans chickpeas, drained and rinsed (see tips)
400 g (14 oz) can cherry tomatoes

1 Combine the oil, lemon juice, rosemary and lemon zest in a shallow glass or ceramic dish. Add the lamb cutlets and turn to coat. Cover and refrigerate for 30 minutes to marinate.

2 Meanwhile, to make the chickpea stew, heat the olive oil in a large saucepan over medium heat. Add the onion and celery and cook, stirring, for 6–7 minutes or until softened. Add the garlic and paprika and cook, stirring, for 1 minute or until fragrant. Stir in the tomato paste and cook for 1 minute. Then add the chickpeas, cherry tomatoes and 80 ml (1/3 cup) water. Bring to the boil, reduce the heat to low and simmer, stirring occasionally, for 10 minutes.

3 Preheat a chargrill pan or barbecue plate over high heat. Drain excess marinade from the cutlets. Grill the cutlets for 2 minutes each side for medium, or until cooked to your liking. Cover loosely with foil and set aside to rest for 2 minutes.

4 Season the chickpeas to taste with sea salt and freshly ground black pepper. Serve with the cutlets and baby spinach leaves.

tips You can replace the canned chickpeas with 450 g (2 2/3 cups) cooked chickpeas.

The stew is suitable to freeze without the cutlets or spinach leaves. Place in an airtight container, cool completely, cover and freeze for up to 2 months.

dairy free

Lamb shoulder lends itself beautifully to slow cooking, becoming rich and meltingly tender. It is high in fat, so it is essential to trim away as much visible fat as you can before cooking, and enjoy this dish only occasionally. I like to serve it with loads of steamed greens to balance the richness of the meat.

Slow-cooked lamb shoulder with caponata

Preparation time: 20 minutes
Cooking time: 2 hours 45 minutes
Serves 6–8

1 tablespoon dijon mustard (see tip)
2 tablespoons balsamic vinegar
1.2 kg (2 lb 11 oz) boneless lamb shoulder, excess fat trimmed
1 tablespoon coarsely chopped rosemary
1 large eggplant (aubergine), cut into 1.5 cm (5/8 inch) dice
1 large red onion, cut into 1.5 cm (5/8 inch) dice
Extra virgin olive oil spray
400 g (14 oz) grape tomatoes, halved
1/2 cup basil leaves, torn
2 tablespoons pine nuts, toasted
2 tablespoons currants
1 tablespoon salted baby capers, rinsed and chopped
2 teaspoons extra virgin olive oil
Steamed greens, to serve

1 Preheat the oven to 220°C (425°F). Mix together the mustard and 1 tablespoon of the vinegar to make a glaze. Place the lamb in a roasting tin, brush evenly with half the mustard glaze and sprinkle with rosemary. Roast for 15 minutes or until browned.

2 Reduce the oven to 160°C (320°F). Place a large piece of baking paper over the lamb, tucking the edges under, then cover the whole tin with a piece of foil. Return to the oven and roast for 2½ hours or until the lamb is so tender that it can be shredded with a fork. Brush the lamb withthe remaining glaze and leave to cool slightly.

3 Meanwhile, place the eggplant and onion on a large tray lined with baking paper and spray with olive oil. Roast for 15 minutes. Add the tomatoes and roast for 10–15 minutes or until the eggplant is golden and tender and the tomatoes are wilted. Transfer to a large bowl and add the basil, pine nuts, currants, capers, olive oil and remaining vinegar. Season to taste with sea salt and freshly ground black pepper.

4 Coarsely shred the lamb and serve hot with the caponata and steamed greens.

tip Dijon mustard should be gluten-free, but always check the label.

(pictured page 158)

dairy free

Boneless lamb loin makes a delicious mini roast, especially when it's served with white bean mash – a creamy, fibre-packed alternative to mashed potato. Fibre is a nutrient that can assist in reducing C-reactive protein, a marker of inflammation.

Lamb loin roast on white bean mash with zucchini salad

Preparation time: 30 minutes
Cooking time: 20 minutes
Serves 4

50 g (1¾ oz) roasted red capsicum (pepper), diced

40 g (1½ oz) baby English spinach leaves, chopped

1 tablespoon chopped oregano

1 tablespoon pine nuts, toasted

500 g (1 lb 2 oz) lamb loin roast, fat trimmed

1 teaspoon extra virgin olive oil

WHITE BEAN MASH

1 teaspoon extra virgin olive oil

1 garlic clove, crushed

1 teaspoon finely grated lemon zest

2 x 400 g (14 oz) cans cannellini beans, rinsed

125 ml (½ cup) homemade or salt-reduced gluten-free chicken stock

1 tablespoon lemon juice, or to taste

ZUCCHINI SALAD

1 tablespoon extra virgin olive oil

1 tablespoon lemon juice

1 teaspoon finely grated lemon zest

3 large zucchini (courgettes)

1 tablespoon each oregano leaves and snipped chives

1 Preheat the oven to 200°C (400°F). Mix together the capsicum, spinach, oregano and pine nuts to make a stuffing.

2 Remove any string from the lamb and unroll the meat. Spread the stuffing between the two long sections of the loin, then re-roll, keeping the skin and fat on the outside. Secure at intervals with kitchen string and brush the lamb with olive oil.

3 Heat a large non-stick frying pan over high heat. Add the lamb and cook for 1–2 minutes each side or until browned. Transfer to a roasting tin and roast until cooked to your liking (20 minutes for medium). Remove from the oven, cover loosely with foil and leave to rest for 10 minutes.

4 Meanwhile, for the white bean mash, heat the olive oil in a saucepan over medium heat. Add the garlic and lemon zest and cook, stirring, for 1 minute or until fragrant. Add the cannellini beans and stock and simmer for 2–3 minutes or until the liquid is reduced by half. Transfer the bean mixture to a food processor and mix until smooth. Add lemon juice to taste and season with sea salt and freshly ground black pepper. Return to a saucepan and stir over medium heat until warmed through.

5 For the zucchini salad, whisk the olive oil, lemon juice, lemon zest in a large bowl. Cut the zucchini into spaghetti-like strands using a spiraliser, or peel it into ribbons with a vegetable peeler. Add the zucchini and herbs to the bowl and gently toss with the dressing. Season to taste with sea salt.

6 Thickly slice the lamb and serve with the white bean mash and zucchini salad.

(pictured page 159)

Slow-cooked lamb shoulder with caponata

(see recipe page 156)

Lamb loin roast on white bean mash with zucchini salad

(see recipe page 157)

dairy free

Spice blends such as dukkah are a great way to add lots of flavour to grilled or roasted meat or tofu. The spice 'seasoning' blends available in supermarkets, however, tend to be high in sodium and other additives, so do check the label or, even better, make your own (see tips).

Dukkah pork with roasted apple and beetroot salad

Preparation time: 15 minutes
Cooking time: 30 minutes
Serves 4

600 g (1 lb 5 oz/2 bunches) baby beetroot (beets), scrubbed, leaves reserved

3 red apples, cored and cut into wedges

Extra virgin olive oil spray

1½ tablespoons balsamic vinegar

2 teaspoons thyme leaves

4 x 100 g (3½ oz) pork loin steaks

1 tablespoon extra virgin olive oil

2 tablespoons dukkah (see tips)

100 g (3½ oz) treviso radicchio, leaves torn (see tips)

50 g (1 cup) baby English spinach leaves or baby kale

1 Preheat the oven to 200°C (400°F) and line a large baking tray with baking paper. Cut the beetroot into halves or quarters and arrange on the tray along with the apple wedges. Spray with olive oil, drizzle with 2 teaspoons of the vinegar and sprinkle with thyme. Roast for 30 minutes or until the beetroot are tender and the apples are golden.

2 Meanwhile, brush the pork with 1 teaspoon of the olive oil and sprinkle both sides with dukkah. Heat a large non-stick frying pan over medium heat. Add the pork and cook for 3–4 minutes each side or until browned and cooked to your liking. Remove, cover loosely with foil and set aside to rest for 5 minutes. Thickly slice.

3 Combine the radicchio and spinach in a large bowl. Add the beetroot, apple, remaining vinegar and remaining olive oil and toss to combine. Serve the pork with the roasted apple and beetroot salad.

tips To make your own dukkah, lightly toast 35g (¼ cup) pistachio kernels or almonds, 1 tablespoon sesame seeds, 2 teaspoons cumin seeds and 2 teaspoons coriander seeds. Pound with 1 teaspoon sea salt in a mortar and pestle until finely ground. This makes more than you'll need for the pork, but the remainder will keep for a month in an airtight container.

Treviso radicchio has elongated leaves and tends to have a milder flavour than the round variety.

I like to swap lasagna sheets with roasted pumpkin for a gluten-free and veggie-packed version of this all-time family favourite. Cottage cheese is significantly lower in saturated fat than regular cheddar cheese, so offers a better choice to traditional béchamel.

Beef and veggie lasagna

Preparation time: 25 minutes
Cooking time: 1 hour
Serves 6

1 kg (2 lb 4 oz) pumpkin (winter squash), peeled, thinly sliced

Extra virgin olive oil spray

1 tablespoon extra virgin olive oil

1 onion, finely chopped

1 large carrot, finely chopped

3 celery stalks, finely chopped

1 small red capsicum (pepper), finely chopped

2 garlic cloves, crushed

1 tablespoon chopped fresh oregano

500 g (1 lb 2 oz) extra-lean minced (ground) beef

2 tablespoons no-added-salt tomato paste (concentrated purée)

400 g (14 oz) can diced tomatoes

3 large zucchini (courgettes), cut into thin ribbons (see tip)

CHEESE SAUCE

300 g (1 cup) cottage cheese

1 egg

60 ml (1/4 cup) reduced-fat milk

1 Preheat the oven to 200°C (400°F). Line 2 large baking trays with baking paper. Place the pumpkin on the trays and lightly spray with oil. Bake for 25–30 minutes or until golden and tender, swapping the trays halfway through cooking.

2 Meanwhile, heat the oil in a large saucepan over medium heat. Cook the onion, carrot, celery and capsicum, stirring occasionally, for 7–8 minutes or until the vegetables are softened. Add the garlic and oregano and cook, stirring, for 1 minute or until fragrant.

3 Add the mince and cook, breaking up any lumps with a wooden spoon, for 5 minutes or until browned. Add the paste and cook, stirring, for 1 minute. Add the tomatoes and 125 ml (1/2 cup) water and bring to the boil. Reduce the heat to low and simmer, stirring occasionally, for 20 minutes, or until thick.

4 Meanwhile, combine the cottage cheese, egg and milk in a bowl. Season with salt and freshly ground black pepper.

5 Lightly spray a 2 litre (8 cup) baking dish with oil. Lay one-half of the zucchini slices over the base of the prepared dish, slightly overlapping. Spread half of the mince mixture over the zucchini. Top with half of the pumpkin. Repeat with another layer of zucchini, mince and pumpkin, then top with the cheese sauce. Bake for 30–35 minutes or until golden brown and bubbling. Set aside to cool slightly for 10 minutes before serving.

tip Cut zucchini ribbons using a vegetable peeler.

dairy free

Adding lentils to this stew is a great way to reduce the quantity of meat – and therefore saturated fat – per serve, yet add a good dose of beneficial dietary fibre and plant protein. Serve with plenty of steamed greens to up the veg content.

Slow cooked beef and lentil stew

Preparation time: 20 minutes
Cooking time: 2 hours
Serves 6

1 tablespoon extra virgin olive oil

600 g (1 lb 5 oz) oyster blade steak, fat trimmed, cut into 2 cm (3/4 inch) cubes

1 large onion, diced

1 large carrot, diced

1 small (about 350 g/12 oz) eggplant (aubergine), cut into 2 cm (3/4 inch) cubes

2 teaspoons ground cumin

1 teaspoon ground coriander

400 g (14 oz) can diced tomatoes

250 ml (1 cup) homemade or salt-reduced gluten-free beef stock

400 g (14 oz) can brown lentils, rinsed and drained

Steamed greens, to serve

1 Preheat the oven to 160°C (320°F). Heat half the oil in a large flameproof heavy-based baking dish over medium–high heat. Cook the beef in 2 batches, turning, for 5 minutes or until browned. Transfer to a heatproof bowl.

2 Heat the remaining oil in the same pan over medium heat. Cook the onion, carrot and eggplant, stirring, for 6–7 minutes or until softened. Add the cumin and coriander and cook, stirring, for 1 minute or until fragrant. Return the beef to the pan with the tomatoes and stock and bring to the boil. Cover and bake in the oven for 1½ hours or until the beef is tender. Add the lentils to the pan and bake, covered, for 15 minutes further.

3 Serve the stew with the steamed greens.

tip This stew is suitable to freeze. Place in individual airtight containers, cool, then cover and freeze for up to 1 month.

dairy free

Marinating the meat before cooking is the secret to these delicious pork satay skewers. Thinly sliced lean rump steak, chicken breast or lamb leg steak would work equally well.

Pork satays with pickled carrot salad

Preparation time: 20 minutes (plus 20 minutes soaking and 1 hour marinating)
Cooking time: 10 minutes
Serves 4

50 g (1/3 cup) unsalted roasted peanuts

2 tablespoons gluten-free salt-reduced soy sauce

1 tablespoon lemon juice

1½ tablespoons gluten-free mirin

1 tablespoon curry powder

1 garlic clove, crushed

500 g (1 lb 2 oz) pork leg steaks, trimmed and cut into long strips

12 short wooden skewers, soaked in cold water for 20 minutes (see tip)

Macadamia oil, for brushing

80 ml (1/3 cup) reduced-fat coconut milk

PICKLED CARROT SALAD

2 tablespoons rice vinegar

2 teaspoons rice malt syrup

2 carrots, peeled and trimmed

2 Lebanese (short) cucumbers, trimmed

1 red appled, cored and cut into thin matchsticks

1/4 cup coriander (cilantro) leaves, roughly chopped

1 Process the peanuts in a food processor until finely chopped. Add the soy sauce, lemon juice, mirin, curry powder and garlic and process until well combined.

2 Transfer half the peanut mixture to a shallow glass or ceramic dish (reserve the remainder). Add the pork and turn to coat. Cover and set aside in the refrigerator to marinate for at least 1 hour.

3 Meanwhile, to begin the pickled carrot salad, combine the rice vinegar, malt syrup and a large pinch of sea salt in a small saucepan and bring to a simmer over medium heat. Remove from the heat and set aside to cool. Transfer to a large bowl. Use a vegetable peeler or mandolin to cut long ribbons or strands from the carrot and cucumber, stopping when you reach the seeds. Add the vegetables to the vinegar mixture and toss to combine. Set aside to pickle for 10 minutes.

4 Thread the pork onto the prepared skewers. Heat a chargrill pan over high heat and brush with oil. Grill the pork skewers, turning, for 4–5 minutes or until lightly charred and cooked to your liking.

5 Meanwhile, combine the remaining peanut mixture with the coconut milk in a small saucepan. Bring to a simmer over medium heat and simmer for 2 minutes or until slightly thickened.

6 Drain the pickling liquid from the vegetables (discard liquid) and toss the vegetables with the apple and coriander. Serve the satays with the peanut sauce and the pickled carrot salad.

tip Soaking wooden skewers in water prevents them from burning. If you're short of time, substitute metal skewers.

vegetables

vegan

Even the most committed meat-eater will love this vegetable stack. The lentils in the tomato sauce add protein, the mushrooms are rich in B vitamins and the cashew 'cheese' is a delicious alternative to a traditional cheese sauce. What's more, the cashews offer a good dose of healthy fats and magnesium.

Roasted vegetable stack with cashew 'cheese'

Preparation time: 30 minutes
Cooking time: 1 hour
Serves 6

850 g (1 lb 14 oz) sweet potato, cut into thin rounds

1 large eggplant (aubergine) (about 550 g/1 lb 4 oz), cut into 5 mm (1/4 inch) slices

Extra virgin olive oil spray

1 tablespoon extra virgin olive oil, plus 1 teaspoon extra for drizzling

1 red onion, finely chopped

200 g (7 oz) mushrooms, sliced

2 garlic cloves, crushed

2 x 400 g (14 oz) cans diced tomatoes

70 g (1/3 cup) red lentils, rinsed

Small handful of basil leaves

3 large zucchini (courgettes)

1 quantity cashew cheese **(see page 222)**

1 Preheat the oven to 200°C (400°F) and line 2 large baking trays with baking paper. Place the sweet potato and the eggplant on the trays and spray with olive oil. Roast for 30 minutes, turning and swapping the trays halfway through cooking, until golden and tender.

2 Meanwhile, heat the olive oil in a large saucepan. Cook the onion, stirring, for 5 minutes or until softened. Add the mushrooms and cook, stirring, for 3–4 minutes or until browned. Add the garlic and stir for 30 seconds. Add the tomatoes, lentils and 170 ml (2/3 cup) water and bring to the boil. Reduce the heat and simmer, partially covered, for 25 minutes or until the lentils are tender and the sauce is thick. Stir in half the basil and season to taste.

3 Cut the zucchini into long ribbons with a vegetable peeler, stopping when you reach the seeds.

4 Lightly spray a 2 litre (8 cup) ovenproof dish with olive oil. Spread 1/2 cup of the tomato mixture in the dish. Arrange a third of the zucchini ribbons in a single layer on top of the tomato.

5 Top with half the eggplant and half the sweet potato. Spread with half the cashew cheese and half the remaining tomato mix.

6 Repeat with half the remaining zucchini and all the remaining eggplant, sweet potato, cashew cheese and tomato mixture.

7 Finish with a layer of zucchini and drizzle with the extra oil. Bake for 20–25 minutes or until bubbling. Leave for 5 minutes before cutting. Garnish with the rest of the basil.

vegetarian

Like all orange and yellow vegetables, sweet potatoes are an excellent source of the powerful antioxidant beta-carotene, which has been linked to a reduced risk of cancer and heart disease, and with potential anti-inflammatory properties.

Baked sweet potatoes stuffed with spinach, feta and pepitas

Preparation time: 15 minutes
Cooking time: 50 minutes
Serves 4

4 small sweet potatoes (about 200 g/7 oz each), scrubbed

1 tablespoon extra virgin olive oil

2 large red onions, thinly sliced

2 garlic cloves, thinly sliced

100 g (2¼ cups) baby English spinach leaves

50 g (1¾ oz) reduced-fat feta cheese, crumbled

2 tablespoons seedless raisins

1 tablespoon pepitas (pumpkin seeds), lightly toasted

1 tablespoon sunflower seeds, lightly toasted

1 Preheat the oven to 200°C (400°F). Prick the sweet potatoes well and roast for 40–50 minutes, turning once, until tender when pierced with a skewer.

2 Meanwhile, heat the olive oil in a large non-stick frying pan over low heat and cook the onion, stirring occasionally, for 8–10 minutes or until softened and light golden. Add the garlic and cook, stirring, for 1 minute. Add the spinach and stir until just wilted. Remove from the heat, add the feta, raisins and seeds and season to taste with sea salt and freshly ground black pepper.

3 Cut a slit in each baked sweet potato. Mash the flesh lightly with a fork and spoon the filling into the sweet potatoes.

This version of the traditional Lebanese dish called *mujadara* contains the winning combo of wholegrain brown rice and lentils, which together make a complete protein. It's delicious as a vegetarian main course or served with grilled fish.

Spiced lentils and rice with spinach and caramelised onions

Preparation time: 15 minutes
Cooking time: 30 minutes
Serves 4

170 g (3/4 cup) brown lentils, rinsed
150 g (3/4 cup) brown rice
2 tablespoons extra virgin olive oil
3 red onions, thinly sliced
2 garlic cloves, crushed
1 teaspoon ground cumin
1 teaspoon ground coriander
150 g (5½ oz) English spinach, coarsely chopped
Lemon juice, to taste
Natural yoghurt, to serve

1 Cook the lentils and rice in a large saucepan of boiling water for 25 minutes or until just tender. Drain well.

2 Meanwhile, heat 1 tablespoon of the oil in a large non-stick frying pan over low heat. Add the onions and cook, stirring occasionally, for 15–20 minutes or until golden and caramelised.

3 Heat the remaining oil in a large saucepan over medium heat. Add the garlic and spices and cook, stirring, for 1 minute or until fragrant. Add half the caramelised onion and cook for 1 minute. Add the rice and lentils and stir to heat through. Stir in the spinach and add lemon juice to taste.

4 Serve the lentils and rice topped with the remaining caramelised onions and a dollop of yoghurt.

vegetarian (see tips)

Cauliflower combined with egg and parmesan makes a fantastic gluten-free alternative to traditional pizza bases.

Cauliflower crust pizza with white beans, pumpkin and cherry tomatoes

Preparation time: 25 minutes
Cooking time: 55 minutes
Makes 2 pizzas

700 g (1 lb 9 oz) butternut pumpkin (squash), peeled, seeded and cut into 1.5 cm (5/8 inch) dice

Extra virgin olive oil spray

1½ tablespoons extra virgin olive oil

1 tablespoon finely chopped mint, plus ¼ cup mint leaves, to serve

2 teaspoons finely chopped rosemary

1 teaspoon finely grated lemon zest, plus extra to serve

45 g (1/3 cup) finely grated mozzarella cheese

400 g (14 oz) can butter beans, drained and rinsed

200 g (7 oz) grape tomatoes, halved

2 tablespoons finely grated parmesan cheese (see tips)

¼ cup flat-leaf (Italian) parsley leaves

CAULIFLOWER CRUST

1 large head (1.2 kg/2 lb 11 oz) cauliflower, trimmed and cut into florets

2 eggs, lightly beaten

35 g (1/3 cup) finely grated parmesan cheese (see tips)

1 garlic clove, crushed

1 Preheat the oven to 220°C (425°F). Line a baking tray and two large pizza trays with baking paper. Place the pumpkin on the baking tray and spray with olive oil to coat. Roast for 25 minutes or until golden and tender.

2 Meanwhile, to make the cauliflower crust, process the cauliflower in batches in a food processor until finely chopped. Transfer to a large microwave-safe bowl and cover with plastic wrap. Microwave on high for 8 minutes or until just tender (see tips). Drain, return to the bowl and cool completely. Stir in the eggs, parmesan and garlic. Divide the mixture in half and press each portion into a 22 cm (8½ inch) circle approximately 3 mm (1/8 inch) thick on the lined pizza tray. Spray with olive oil and bake for 15 minutes or until the edges are golden.

3 Combine the oil, chopped herbs and lemon zest in a bowl. Brush the crusts with the oil mixture, sprinkle with the mozzarella and top with the beans, tomatoes, roasted pumpkin and parmesan. Bake the pizzas, swapping the trays halfway through cooking, for 12 minutes or until golden.

4 Meanwhile, combine the mint leaves, extra lemon zest and parsley in a small bowl. Scatter over the pizzas and serve.

tips Microwaving the cauliflower gives the best results for this recipe. It's not necessary to add any water, but it's important to cover the cauliflower so it steams. Alternatively, you can steam the cauliflower, covered, over simmering water on the stovetop for 8 minutes or until just tender, then drain and cool.

For a vegetarian version, use parmesan made with non-animal rennet.

vegetarian (see tip)

This risotto uses a mix of rice and quinoa to make it more nutritious. Quinoa is a good source of protein and is rich in dietary fibre, which is linked to a reduced risk of cardiovascular disease, cancer and type 2 diabetes. It is also high in manganese, and a good source of phosphorus, magnesium and folate.

Quinoa risotto with beans, lemon and parmesan

Preparation time: 15 minutes
Cooking time: 35 minutes
Serves 4

- **300 g (10½ oz) podded fresh or frozen broad (fava) beans**
- **1 litre (4 cups) homemade or salt-reduced gluten-free vegetable stock**
- **1 tablespoon extra virgin olive oil**
- **1 leek, white part only, thinly sliced**
- **2 garlic cloves, crushed**
- **2 teaspoons thyme leaves**
- **150 g (⅔ cup) arborio rice**
- **100 g (½ cup) white quinoa, rinsed and drained**
- **80 ml (⅓ cup) white wine**
- **140 g (1 cup) podded fresh or frozen green peas**
- **25 g (¼ cup) finely grated parmesan cheese, plus extra to serve (see tip)**
- **1 teaspoon finely grated lemon zest**
- **Mint leaves, to garnish**

1 Cook the broad beans in a saucepan of boiling water for 1 minute. Refresh under cold running water. Drain. Peel off the skins and discard. Set aside.

2 Put the stock in a large saucepan and bring to the boil. Reduce the heat to low and keep the stock at a simmer.

3 Heat the oil in a large heavy-based saucepan over medium heat. Add the leek and cook, stirring, for 5 minutes or until soft. Add the garlic and thyme leaves and cook, stirring, for 1 minute or until fragrant. Add the rice and white quinoa and stir for 1–2 minutes or until the grains are well coated in the oil. Add the wine and simmer until reduced by half.

4 Gradually add the simmering stock, a cup at a time, stirring constantly and making sure the stock is absorbed before you add more. This will take 15–20 minutes; the rice should be al dente yet creamy.

5 Stir in the peas and broad beans. Simmer for 2–3 minutes or until the vegetables are just tender, then remove from the heat and stir in the parmesan and lemon zest. Cover and set aside for 3 minutes. Season to taste with sea salt and freshly ground black pepper. Serve garnished with mint and extra parmesan.

tip For a vegetarian version, use parmesan made with non-animal rennet.

vegan (see tips)

Purple carrots might seem exotic, but in fact they're thought to predate the regular orange variety. They gain their colour from anthocyanin, pigments that act as powerful antioxidants in the body with anti-inflammatory properties.

Roasted carrots and asparagus with lemon, honey and thyme dressing

Preparation time: 10 minutes
Cooking time: 30 minutes
Serves 4 as a side dish

500 g (1 lb 2 oz) baby carrots, scrubbed and halved lengthways (see tips)

1 tablespoon extra virgin olive oil

1 tablespoon single origin floral honey (see tips)

2 teaspoons lemon juice

1 garlic clove, crushed

2 teaspoons chopped thyme leaves

2 bunches asparagus (about 16 spears)

1 Preheat the oven to 200°C (400°F). Line a large baking tray with baking paper. Toss the carrots with the olive oil, season with sea salt and freshly ground black pepper and arrange on the tray. Roast for 20 minutes.

2 Mix together the honey, lemon juice, garlic and thyme.

3 Add the asparagus to the carrots. Drizzle with the dressing and toss to coat well. Roast for 10 minutes or until golden and tender. Serve hot or at room temperature.

tips A combination of yellow, orange and purple carrots makes an especially colourful dish.

For a vegan version, replace the honey with maple syrup.

(pictured page 180)

vegetarian (see tip)

When it comes to barbecuing, nothing beats sweet corn, especially when it's teamed with lime and smoky paprika. Antioxidant carotenoids, lutein and zeaxanthin all promote healthy eyesight, and corn is packed with them. It's also rich in dietary fibre, which promotes a healthy bowel.

Barbecued corn with lime and smoked paprika

Preparation time: 10 minutes
Cooking time: 10 minutes
Serves 4 as a side dish

Extra virgin olive oil spray
1 teaspoon smoked paprika
1 teaspoon finely grated lime zest
¼ teaspoon chilli flakes
25 g (¼ cup) finely grated pecorino cheese (see tip)
1 tablespoon macadamia oil
4 cobs corn, husks and silks removed
Lime wedges, to serve

1 Preheat a barbecue or chargrill pan to medium heat. Cut four 30 cm (12 inch) squares of foil and spray each piece with olive oil.

2 Mix together the paprika, lime zest, chilli and 2 tablespoons of the pecorino. Put each corn cob on a square of foil. Brush the corn cobs with macadamia oil, then sprinkle with the paprika mixture. Season each cob with sea salt and freshly ground black pepper and wrap up in foil.

3 Barbecue the corn parcels, turning occasionally, for 8–10 minutes or until the corn is lightly charred and tender. Serve sprinkled with the remaining pecorino, with lime wedges on the side.

tip For a vegetarian version, use pecorino (or parmesan) made with non-animal rennet.

(pictured page 181)

Roasted carrots and asparagus with lemon, honey and thyme dressing

(see recipe page 178)

Barbecued corn with lime and smoked paprika

(see recipe page 179)

Stir-fried broccolini and green beans with spicy seeds

(see recipe page 182)

vegan

Macadamia oil is perfect for stir-fries because it has a high smoke point (the temperature at which a cooking oil begins to break down); its delicious nutty taste is a bonus. It's also extremely rich in healthy monounsaturated fats.

Stir-fried broccolini and green beans with spicy seeds

Preparation time: 10 minutes
Cooking time: 10 minutes
Serves 4 as a side dish

1 tablespoon macadamia oil
360 g (12¾ oz) broccolini
200 g (7 oz) green beans
1 tablespoon pepitas (pumpkin seeds)
1 tablespoon sunflower seeds
4 garlic cloves, thinly sliced
1 teaspoon finely grated lemon zest
¼ teaspoon chilli flakes

1 Heat half the oil in a wok or large frying pan over high heat and stir-fry the broccolini and beans for 3–4 minutes or until just tender. Remove from the wok.

2 Reduce the heat to medium. Add the remaining oil and the seeds and stir-fry for 2 minutes or until golden. Add the garlic, lemon zest and chilli and stir-fry for 30 seconds or until aromatic.

3 Return the broccolini and beans to the wok and stir-fry for 1 minute to heat through. Serve immediately.

(pictured page 181)

vegetarian • dairy free

The soy bean is one of the few plant foods that is a complete protein: it contains all the essential amino acids. These burgers, with their combination of soy beans and quinoa, are packed with protein, fibre and anti-inflammatory phytonutrients. Win–win–win!

Quinoa bean burgers with fresh beetroot slaw

Preparation time: 25 minutes
Cooking time: 25 minutes
Serves 4

- 1½ tablespoons extra virgin olive oil
- 1 onion, finely chopped
- 1 tablespoon gluten-free korma curry paste
- 65 g (⅓ cup) quinoa, rinsed and drained
- 400 g (14 oz) can soy beans, drained and rinsed (see tips)
- 1 small carrot, peeled and finely grated
- 2 tablespoons finely chopped mixed soft herbs, such as parsley, mint and coriander (cilantro)
- 2 tablespoons sunflower seeds
- 30 g (⅓ cup) quinoa flakes
- 4 gluten-free or wholegrain burger buns, halved and toasted
- 2 tablespoons hummus
- Baby rocket (arugula) leaves, to serve

BEETROOT SLAW

- 1 tablespoon red wine vinegar
- 2 teaspoons single origin floral honey
- 2 beetroot (beets), peeled and coarsely grated
- 1 small green apple, coarsely grated

1 Heat 2 teaspoons of the olive oil in a saucepan over medium heat. Cook the onion, stirring, for 5 minutes or until softened. Add the curry paste and cook, stirring, for 30 seconds or until fragrant. Add the quinoa and 170 ml (⅔ cup) water and bring to the boil. Reduce the heat to low, cover and simmer for 10–12 minutes or until the water has evaporated and the quinoa is just tender. Set aside to cool completely.

2 Mash the soy beans in a large bowl, leaving a little texture. Add the quinoa, carrot, herbs and sunflower seeds and mix until well combined. Shape into 4 patties. Place the quinoa flakes on a large plate and press each patty into the flakes to coat on all sides.

3 Heat the remaining olive oil in a large non-stick frying pan over medium heat. Cook the burgers for 3 minutes each side or until golden and crisp.

4 Meanwhile, to make the beetroot slaw, combine the red wine vinegar, honey in a bowl. Add the beetroot and apple and stir until well combined.

5 Spread the burger buns with hummus. Fill each bun with rocket leaves, a burger and beetroot slaw and serve.

tips It is important to cook the quinoa until all the water has evaporated to ensure the burgers are not too wet.

You can replace the canned soy beans with 225 g (1⅓ cups) cooked soy beans or another type of canned legume, such as four-bean mix, chickpeas or cannellini beans.

vegetarian

Of all the legumes, lentils are among the highest in protein. Combined with quinoa, they make a high-protein dish that's packed with flavour.

Lentil and quinoa pilaf with roasted vegetables

Preparation time: 15 minutes
Cooking time: 40 minutes
Serves 4

110 g (1/2 cup) dried brown or green lentils, rinsed and drained

1/2 small head cauliflower, trimmed and cut into florets

1 red capsicum (pepper), seeded and sliced

Extra virgin olive oil spray

300 g (10 1/2 oz) broccoli, trimmed and cut into florets

1 tablespoon extra virgin olive oil

1 onion, finely chopped

2 garlic cloves, crushed

1 teaspoon cumin seeds, crushed

1 cinnamon stick

250 ml (1 cup) homemade or salt-reduced gluten-free vegetable stock

100 g (1/2 cup) quinoa, rinsed and drained

1/4 cup coarsely chopped flat-leaf (Italian) parsley

Natural yoghurt, to serve

2 tablespoons pistachio kernels, coarsely chopped

Thinly sliced lemon zest, to garnish

1 Place the lentils in a saucepan and cover with cold water. Bring to the boil, then reduce the heat to medium–low and simmer for 20–25 minutes or until tender. Drain.

2 Meanwhile, preheat the oven to 200°C (400°F). Line a large baking tray with baking paper. Put the cauliflower and capsicum on the tray and spray lightly with olive oil. Roast for 10 minutes. Add the broccoli to the tray and spray with a little more oil. Roast for 10 minutes or until the vegetables are golden and tender. Set aside.

3 Heat the oil in a large saucepan over medium heat. Add the onion and cook, stirring, for 5 minutes or until light golden. Add the garlic, cumin and cinnamon and cook, stirring, for 1 minute or until fragrant. Add the stock and quinoa and bring to the boil. Cover and simmer for 12–15 minutes or until the stock has been absorbed and the quinoa is al dente. Stir in the lentils and parsley.

4 Serve the lentil and quinoa pilaf topped with the roasted vegetables and a dollop of yoghurt, garnished with pistachios and a little lemon zest.

vegetarian (see tip)

When I first heard millet could be used to make a soft polenta-like dish, I was sceptical. However, I could not believe the end result — creamy, rich and best of all, unlike polenta, millet does not become stiff after sitting in the dish. The trick is to cook it slowly with a higher ratio of liquid than usual.

Creamy parmesan millet with ratatouille

Preparation time: 20 minutes
Cooking time: 50 minutes
Serves 4

210 g (1 cup) hulled millet

500 ml (2 cups) homemade or salt-reduced gluten-free vegetable stock

25 g (1/4 cup) grated parmesan cheese, plus extra, to serve (see tip)

RATATOUILLE

2 tablespoons extra virgin olive oil

1 red onion, diced

2 garlic cloves, crushed

1 red capsicum (pepper), seeded and diced

2 zucchini (courgettes), diced

1 small eggplant (aubergine), diced

400 g (14 oz) can chopped tomatoes

2 teaspoons thyme leaves

1 Heat a large saucepan over medium–high heat, add the millet and cook, stirring, for 3 minutes or until fragrant.

2 Add the stock and 500 ml (2 cups) water to the millet and bring to the boil. Reduce the heat to low, cover and simmer, stirring occasionally, for 45 minutes or until thick and creamy. Add a little extra water during cooking if it looks too dry. Stir in the parmesan and season well.

3 Meanwhile, to make the ratatouille, heat the olive oil in a large saucepan. Add the onion and cook, stirring occasionally, for 5 minutes or until softened. Add the garlic and stir for 1 minute more.

4 Increase the heat to high, add the capsicum, zucchini and eggplant and cook, stirring occasionally, for 5 minutes. Add the tomatoes and thyme, reduce the heat to low and simmer for 10 minutes or until the vegetables are tender, adding a little water if the sauce is becoming too thick. Season to taste.

5 Serve the parmesan millet in shallow bowls, topped with ratatouille and sprinkled with grated parmesan.

tip For a vegetarian version, use parmesan made with non-animal rennet.

vegan

Chia seeds work just like sesame seeds in this delicious dukkah. They also add dietary fibre, essential fatty acids and protein. Just add a leafy salad and a slice of gluten-free or wholegrain bread to make this a complete meal, or serve as a warm vegetable side.

Roasted root vegetables with chia dukkah

Preparation time: 25 minutes
Cooking time: 45 minutes
Serves 4

6 medium beetroot (beets) (about 700 g/1 lb 9 oz in total), peeled and cut into wedges

2 large parsnips (about 400 g/14 oz in total), peeled and cut into thick batons

1 large bunch Dutch (baby) carrots (about 500 g/1 lb 2 oz in total), trimmed, scrubbed and halved lengthways if large

2 tablespoons extra virgin olive oil, plus extra, to drizzle

CHIA DUKKAH

1 tablespoon coriander seeds

1 tablespoon cumin seeds

70 g (½ cup) pistachio kernels, lightly toasted

2 tablespoons white chia seeds

2 teaspoons sea salt

1 Preheat the oven to 200°C (400°F). Put the vegetables in a single layer on a large baking tray lined with baking paper. Drizzle with the olive oil and season with sea salt and freshly ground black pepper. Roast the vegetables for 40–45 minutes or until tender.

2 Meanwhile, to make the chia dukkah, put the coriander and cumin seeds in a small dry frying pan over medium–high heat. Cook, stirring, for 2–3 minutes or until fragrant. Transfer to a mortar and pound with the pestle until finely crushed.

3 Put the toasted spices, pistachios, chia seeds and salt in a small food processor and process until finely chopped.

4 To serve, pile the roasted vegetables onto a serving platter, sprinkle with the chia dukkah and drizzle with a little extra olive oil.

tip The dukkah will keep, stored in an airtight container, for up to 1 month. Try sprinkling it over grilled (broiled) meats (such as lamb cutlets, chicken or beef) or grilled pitta or Turkish bread as part of a mezze plate.

sweet treats

dairy free

Packed with sweet dried fruit, this cake doesn't need any added sugar, and the mashed pumpkin keeps it deliciously moist. Glacé ginger adds spice, as well as the chemicals gingerol and shogaol, with anti-inflammatory properties. It's very rich, so just a small piece will leave you feeling satisfied.

Almond, date and cranberry cake

Preparation time: 15 minutes
Cooking time: 1 hour 20 minutes
Makes 24 small pieces

150 g (1 cup) seedless raisins
150 g (1 cup) sweetened dried cranberries
150 g (1 cup) pitted dates, chopped
185 ml (3/4 cup) fresh orange juice
200 g (2 cups) almond meal
100 g (1/2 cup) glacé ginger, chopped
1 teaspoon ground cinnamon
1 teaspoon mixed spice
Finely grated zest of 1 orange
125 g (1/2 cup) mashed pumpkin (winter squash; see tips)
2 eggs, lightly beaten
2 tablespoons macadamia oil
1 teaspoon natural vanilla extract

1 Preheat the oven to 160°C (325°F). Grease the base and sides of a 20 cm (8 inch) square cake tin and line with baking paper.

2 Combine the raisins, cranberries, dates and orange juice in a saucepan and bring just to the boil. Set aside to cool.

3 Combine the almond meal, ginger, cinnamon, mixed spice and orange zest in a large bowl and make a well in the centre. Mix together the pumpkin, eggs, oil, vanilla and soaked fruit and pour into the well. Stir well.

4 Spoon into the tin and smooth the surface with the back of a spoon. Bake for 1 hour 15 minutes or until the cake is golden, the top firm and a skewer poked into the centre comes out clean. If it browns too quickly, cover with foil. Cool completely in the tin, before cutting into 24 pieces.

tips You'll need about 150 g (5½ oz) peeled raw pumpkin to make ½ cup cooked mashed pumpkin.

Store in an airtight container in a cool dark place for up to 2 weeks.

vegan (see tips)

Avocado makes this mousse deliciously creamy, without any cream! Even better, it's rich in monounsaturated fats and contains beta-sitosterol, a plant sterol that helps reduce cholesterol absorption, and the antioxidant vitamin E, a nutrient with anti-inflammatory effects.

Raw chocolate and mesquite mousse

Preparation time: 10 minutes
Cooking time: Nil
Serves 4

2 ripe avocados, stone removed, peeled (see tips)

90 g (1/4 cup) single origin floral honey

30 g (1/4 cup) unsweetened cocoa or raw cacao powder, sifted

2 tablespoons mesquite powder, plus extra to garnish

90 g (1/3 cup) reduced-fat coconut cream

1 Process the avocado, honey, cocoa and mesquite powder in a food processor until smooth. Add the coconut cream and process until smooth and creamy, adding a little extra coconut cream if the mousse is too thick.

2 Spoon the mousse into 4 serving dishes. Cover and refrigerate until chilled. Garnish with a little extra mesquite powder and serve.

tips For a smooth and luscious texture, it's essential to use ripe avocados in this recipe.

For a vegan version, you can replace the honey with rice malt syrup. You may need to add a few extra teaspoons because it is not as sweet as honey.

dairy free (see tips)

The cooked quinoa gives this cake a delicious moist texture. Macadamia oil is ideal for baking as it has a mild and nutty taste and is packed with healthy monounsaturated fatty acids (over 80%!). You can skip the frosting if you wish – the cake is just as delicious with a dusting of extra cinnamon.

Carrot quinoa cake with cream cheese frosting

Preparation time: 20 minutes
Cooking time: 50 minutes
Serves 12

225 g (1½ cups) gluten-free or wholemeal self-raising flour

1 teaspoon ground cinnamon

½ teaspoon ground nutmeg

75 g (½ cup) coconut sugar

50 g (½ cup) almond meal

185 g (1 cup) cooked quinoa

235 g (1½ cups, firmly packed) grated carrot

85 g (½ cup) seedless raisins, coarsely chopped

125 ml (½ cup) macadamia oil

4 eggs

FROSTING (optional)

250 g (9 oz) cream cheese, softened

1 teaspoon finely grated orange zest

1 tablespoon pure maple syrup

2 tablespoons freshly squeezed orange juice, strained

1 Preheat the oven to 180°C (350°F). Grease a 20 cm (8 inch) square cake tin and line with baking paper.

2 Sift the flour, cinnamon and nutmeg together into a large mixing bowl. Add the coconut sugar, almond meal, quinoa, carrot and raisins and stir to combine. Whisk the oil and eggs together, add to the quinoa mixture and stir until well combined.

3 Spoon the batter into the tin and bake for 50 minutes or until the cake is firm to touch and a skewer inserted into the centre comes out with only a few moist crumbs clinging to it. (You may need to cover the cake with foil if it is browning too quickly.) Transfer the tin to a wire rack and set aside to cool for 15 minutes. Remove the cake from the tin and set aside on the wire rack to cool completely.

4 To make the frosting, use an electric mixer to beat the cream cheese and orange zest until smooth. Add the maple syrup and orange juice and beat until well combined. Spread evenly over the top and sides of the cooled carrot cake and serve.

tips Without the frosting, this recipe is dairy free.

This cake will keep, stored in an airtight container in a cool place, for up to 3 days.

dairy free

In this healthy, gluten-free twist on a traditional fruit crumble, fresh plums are topped with a crunchy mixture of almonds and wholegrain buckwheat. The monounsaturated fats in the almonds may lower some markers of inflammation, as well as being rich in the antioxidant vitamin E.

Baked plums with almonds and buckwheat

Preparation time: 10 minutes
Cooking time: 20 minutes
Serves 4

6 firm ripe plums (about 500 g/ 1 lb 2 oz), halved (see tips)

2 tablespoons almond meal

1 tablespoon chilled coconut oil

25 g (1/4 cup) flaked almonds

2 tablespoons buckwheat kernels

1 tablespoon coconut sugar

1 teaspoon ground cinnamon

1 Preheat the oven to 180°C (350°F). Place the plums in a large roasting tin, cut side up (see tips).

2 Place the almond meal in a bowl. Using your fingertips, rub in the oil until the mixture resembles breadcrumbs. Add the remaining ingredients and stir until well combined.

3 Sprinkle the crumble over the plums. Bake for 15–20 minutes or until the plums are soft and the crumble is golden brown.

tips You can replace the plums with another type of stone fruit – nectarines, peaches and apricots all work well.

Lining the tin with baking paper makes washing up easier, but it's not essential.

(pictured page 200)

vegetarian

Poached pears make an easy, healthy dessert, especially if you keep the added sugar to a minimum. They're rich in soluble and insoluble fibre and a good source of vitamin C. Serve them with ricotta combined with natural yoghurt for a healthier alternative to cream or ice cream.

Poached pears with orange, star anise and vanilla ricotta

Preparation time: 10 minutes
Cooking time: 30 minutes
Serves 4

90 g (1/4 cup) single origin floral honey

Juice and thinly peeled zest of 2 oranges

3 star anise

4 firm ripe pears, halved and cored

95 g (1/3 cup) natural yoghurt

80 g (1/3 cup) ricotta cheese

1/2 teaspoon natural vanilla extract

1 Combine the honey, orange juice, orange zest, star anise and 500 ml (2 cups) water in a saucepan over medium heat and stir. Bring to the boil, then reduce the heat to low and simmer for 5 minutes.

2 Add the pears, cover them closely with a piece of baking paper and poach for 15–20 minutes or until tender (the timing will depend on the ripeness of the pears). Remove the pears with a slotted spoon and set aside. Simmer the syrup until reduced by half.

3 Meanwhile, stir together the yoghurt, ricotta and vanilla.

4 To serve, spoon the pears into bowls, drizzle with a little syrup and top with a dollop of vanilla ricotta.

tip The pears and syrup will keep in an airtight container in the refrigerator for up to 3 days. They're delicious served warm or cold.

(pictured page 201)

Poached pears with orange, star anise and vanilla ricotta

(see recipe page 199)

Baked plums with almonds and buckwheat

(see recipe page 198)

dairy free (see tips)

This cake is made from ground hazelnuts, buckwheat flour and macadamia oil, so it's brimming with healthy fatty acids. Buckwheat is a nutritious whole grain, rich in manganese and magnesium.

Hazelnut and raspberry cake

Preparation time: 15 minutes
Cooking time: 45 minutes
Serves 12

45 g (1/3 cup) buckwheat flour
1 teaspoon gluten-free baking powder
1 teaspoon ground cinnamon
1/4 teaspoon ground nutmeg
4 eggs
75 g (1/2 cup) coconut sugar
200 g (7 oz) hazelnut meal
80 ml (1/3 cup) macadamia oil
Finely grated zest of 1 lemon
120 g (1 cup) raspberries, plus extra to serve
Chopped toasted hazelnuts, to serve
Natural yoghurt, to serve (see tips)

1 Preheat the oven to 170°C (340°F). Lightly grease and line a 22 cm (8½ inch) round spring-form cake tin with baking paper.

2 Sift together the flour, baking powder and spices.

3 Use an electric mixer to beat the eggs and coconut sugar until pale and thick. Fold in the spiced flour mixture, hazelnut meal, oil, lemon zest and half the raspberries.

4 Spoon into the tin and decorate the top with the remaining raspberries. Bake for 40–45 minutes or until golden and a skewer poked into the centre comes out clean. If the cake browns too quickly, cover the top with foil. Cool in the tin for 10 minutes, then remove the sides of the tin and cool completely on a wire rack.

5 Scatter with hazelnuts and extra raspberries and serve with yoghurt.

tips For a dairy-free version, serve the cake with coconut yoghurt.

This will keep in an airtight container in a cool dark place for 4 days.

vegetarian

I love something small and sweet after dinner and these choc bites are perfect. They're filled with crunchy puffed amaranth, coconut, almonds and bitter orange, and they're just the right size. To maximise the antioxidant benefits, use a dark chocolate that contains at least 70 per cent cocoa solids.

Amaranth, orange and dark chocolate bites

Preparation time: 15 minutes (plus 4 hours setting)
Cooking time: 5 minutes
Makes about 20

55 g (3/4 cup) shredded coconut

25 g (1/4 cup) flaked natural almonds

20 g (3/4 cup) puffed amaranth

200 g (7 oz) dark chocolate (minimum 70% cocoa solids), coarsely chopped

Thinly peeled zest of 1 orange, white pith removed, finely chopped

1 Lightly toast the coconut, almonds and puffed amaranth in a large frying pan over medium heat for 2–3 minutes. Set aside to cool.

2 Melt the chocolate by stirring in a heatproof bowl over a saucepan of gently simmering water (don't let the base of the bowl touch the water). Remove from the heat. Stir in the amaranth mixture and half the orange zest.

3 Line a large tray with baking paper. Spoon heaped teaspoons of the mixture onto the tray, then sprinkle the mounds with the remaining orange zest.

4 Set aside at room temperature for about 4 hours to set.

tip These choc bites will keep in an airtight container in a cool dark place for up to 1 month.

dairy free

These cupcakes are so simple to make, and they taste amazing. They have a lovely moist texture, and you cannot taste the beans. They are packed with protein and dietary fibre and contain no added oil or butter.

Vanilla almond cakes

Preparation time: 10 minutes
Cooking time: 20 minutes
Makes 10

400 g (14 oz) can cannellini beans, drained and rinsed (see tips)

3 eggs

125 g (1¼ cups) almond meal

75 g (½ cup) coconut sugar

2 teaspoons gluten-free baking powder

2 teaspoons natural vanilla extract

Sifted unsweetened cocoa powder, to garnish

1 Preheat the oven to 180°C (350°F). Line 10 holes of a 12-hole standard (80 ml/⅓ cup) muffin tin with paper cases.

2 Process the beans in a food processor until smooth, scraping down the side of the bowl if necessary. Add the eggs one at a time and process until smooth. Add the almond meal, coconut sugar, baking powder and vanilla. Process again until well combined.

3 Divide the mixture among the paper cases. Bake for 15–20 minutes or until light golden and firm to touch. Transfer to a wire rack to cool for 5 minutes, remove from the tin and set aside on the wire rack to cool completely. Serve dusted with cocoa powder.

tips You can replace the canned cannellini beans with 240 g (1⅓ cups) cooked cannellini beans.

These cupcakes are suitable to freeze. Cool completely then wrap individually in plastic wrap and freeze for up to 1 month.

vegetarian

These more-ish little cookies are packed with fibre and good oils. They're the perfect thing to have with a coffee or cup of tea. Or, try crumbling and layering them in short glasses with natural yoghurt and anti-inflammatory berries for a simple and delicious dessert.

Chia seed Italian cookies

Preparation time: 20 minutes
Cooking time: 20 minutes
Makes 36

2 egg whites, at room temperature
100 g (2/3 cup) coconut sugar
100 g (1 cup) almond meal
100 g (3½ oz) dark chocolate (minimum 70% cocoa solids), chopped
90 g (½ cup) black chia seeds
75 g (½ cup) sesame seeds

1 Preheat the oven to 140°C (275°F). Line 2 large baking trays with baking paper.

2 Use an electric mixer with a whisk attachment to whisk the egg whites in a large bowl until firm peaks form. With the motor running, gradually add 75 g (½ cup) of the coconut sugar, a spoonful at a time, whisking until it is dissolved. Combine the almond meal and the remaining sugar. Fold the almond mixture, chocolate, chia and sesame seeds through the egg white mixture.

3 Spoon 2 teaspoonfuls of the mixture per biscuit onto the lined trays, leaving 4 cm (1½ inches) between each to allow for spreading. Bake for 25 minutes, swapping the trays halfway through cooking, or until just golden and crisp. Remove and set aside on the trays to cool completely. Cookies will continue to crisp as they cool.

tip These cookies will keep in an airtight container for up to 1 week.

vegetarian

Adzuki beans add richness and body as well as a good dose of dietary fibre and protein to these brownies. Macadamia oil is a healthy swap for butter; it has the highest monounsaturated fat content of any oil, and adds a delicious nutty taste.

Double choc bean brownies

Preparation time: 20 minutes
Cooking time: 35 minutes
Makes 16

150 g (5½ oz) dark chocolate (minimum 70% cocoa solids), coarsely chopped

80 ml (⅓ cup) macadamia oil

400 g (14 oz) can adzuki beans, drained and rinsed (see tip)

2 eggs

1 teaspoon natural vanilla extract

2 tablespoons unsweetened cocoa powder, plus extra for dusting

75 g (½ cup) coconut sugar

35 g (⅓ cup) almond or hazelnut meal

1 Preheat the oven to 160°C (320°F). Lightly grease a 20 cm (8 inch) square cake tin and line the base with baking paper.

2 Put 75 g (2¾ oz) of the chocolate and the macadamia oil in a heatproof bowl over a saucepan of gently simmering water. Stir until melted and smooth. Set aside to cool.

3 Process the adzuki beans in a food processor until smooth. Add the eggs and vanilla and process until well combined. Transfer to a large bowl.

4 Stir the chocolate mixture into the bean mixture, then sift the cocoa over the mixture and stir until well combined. Stir in the coconut sugar, nut meal and remaining chopped chocolate.

5 Pour the mixture into the tin. Bake for 30–35 minutes or until just firm when lightly pressed. Set aside to cool in the tin before cutting into squares. Serve dusted with extra cocoa.

tip You can replace the canned adzuki beans with 240 g (1⅓ cups) cooked adzuki beans, red kidney beans or black beans.

dairy free

Chickpeas in a cake may sound strange, but this cake is absolutely delicious. The chickpeas add a nutty taste, texture and body, and the cake does not contain any oil or butter.

Mandarin, pistachio and chickpea cake

Preparation time: 20 minutes
Cooking time: 1 hour 50 minutes
Serves 12

3 mandarins, unpeeled

150 g (1 cup) pistachio kernels, plus 1 tablespoon extra, coarsely chopped, to garnish

400 g (14 oz) can chickpeas, drained and rinsed (see tips)

175 g (½ cup) single origin floral honey

4 eggs

75 g (½ cup) gluten-free or whole meal plain (all-purpose) flour

1 teaspoon gluten-free baking powder

Icing (confectioners') sugar, for dusting (optional)

1 Place the mandarins in a large saucepan, cover with cold water and bring to the boil, then drain. Cover with cold water again, return to the boil, then reduce the heat to low and simmer for 45 minutes, adding a little more water to the pan as necessary. Drain the mandarins and set aside to cool.

2 Preheat the oven to 170°C (325°F). Lightly grease a 22 cm (8½ inch) round cake tin and line it with baking paper.

3 Cut the mandarins into quarters, remove the seeds and discard. Process the pistachios in a food processor to fine crumbs. Remove; set aside. Add the chickpeas to the food processor and process to fine crumbs. Add the mandarins and process until smooth.

4 Use an electric mixer to whisk the honey and eggs in a large bowl until thick. Add the mandarin mixture and fold in until well combined, then add the ground pistachios, flour and baking powder and stir until well combined. Spoon the batter into the tin and smooth the surface with the back of the spoon.

5 Bake for 50 minutes or until a skewer inserted into the centre comes out with a few moist crumbs. If the cake browns too quickly, cover the top loosely with foil. Set aside to cool for 20 minutes, then carefully remove from the tin and cool completely on a wire rack. Serve dusted with icing sugar and garnished with extra chopped pistachios.

tips You can replace the canned chickpeas with 225 g (1⅓ cups) cooked chickpeas.

This cake will keep in an airtight container for up to 3 days.

vegetarian

This version of an old favourite is made from whole foods such as walnuts, dates, coconut and cacao. Walnuts are rich in alpha linoleic acid, a type of anti-inflammatory omega-3 fatty acid, which research shows may lower C-reactive protein, and therefore reduce the risk of arthritis.

Peanut butter cups

Preparation time: 25 minutes
Cooking time: 5 minutes
Makes 24

150 g (5½ oz) dark chocolate (minimum 70% cocoa solids), coarsely chopped

2 teaspoons coconut oil

BASE

60 g (½ cup) walnut halves

25 g (¼ cup) desiccated (shredded) coconut

2 tablespoons raw cacao or unsweetened cocoa powder

125 g (½ cup) medjool dates, pitted

2 teaspoons coconut oil

PEANUT FILLING

75 g (⅓ cup) medjool dates, pitted

215 g (¾ cup) crunchy peanut butter

3 teaspoons single origin floral honey

1 Line a 24-hole mini-muffin tin with paper cases.

2 To make the base, process the walnuts, coconut and cacao in a food processor until finely chopped. With the motor running, add the dates a few at a time. Process until the mixture starts to come together. Add the coconut oil and process until well combined. Press a rounded teaspoon of mixture into the base of each paper case, smoothing the surface with the back of a spoon. Chill until firm.

3 To make the peanut filling, put the dates in a food processor and pulse until finely chopped. Add the peanut butter, honey and a pinch of sea salt and process until smooth. Spoon a little peanut butter mixture into each paper case and smooth the surface. Freeze until firm.

4 Put the chocolate and coconut oil in a heatproof bowl over a saucepan of gently simmering water. Stir until melted and smooth. Spread a little chocolate mixture into each paper case and smooth the surface. Refrigerate until set. Serve chilled.

tip Store the peanut butter cups in an airtight container in the refrigerator. They will keep for up to 2 weeks.

vegan (see tip)

This salad makes a light, refreshing breakfast or dessert when citrus fruits are in season. Feel free to add a handful of chopped nuts or seeds for protein and healthy fats.

Citrus salad with yoghurt, pomegranate and mint

Preparation time: 10 minutes
Cooking time: None
Serves 2

2 ruby red grapefruit
2 navel oranges or blood oranges
1 lime
1 teaspoon coconut sugar
1 tablespoon pomegranate seeds
2 tablespoons small mint leaves
130 g (½ cup) natural or thick coconut yoghurt

1 Remove the skin and pith from the citrus fruit using a small sharp knife. Slice the fruit into thin rounds and arrange on serving plates.

2 Sprinkle with the coconut sugar and top with the pomegranate seeds and mint. Serve with yoghurt.

tip This salad is vegan if you use coconut yoghurt.

vegan

These truffles have a delicious silky texture and you won't believe they're not made from chocolate. Pistachio nuts can help lower LDL cholesterol and are high in the antioxidants vitamin E, Vitamin A and lutein.

Carob, pistachio and date truffles

Preparation time: 15 minutes
Cooking time: None
Makes 30

70 g (½ cup) raw pistachio kernels

2 tablespoons carob powder (see tips)

2 tablespoons almond, brazil nut and cashew butter (ABC nut butter)

240 g (1 cup) Medjool dates, pitted

1 Process ¼ cup of the pistachios in a food processor until finely chopped, then transfer to a large plate.

2 Process the carob powder and the remaining pistachios in the food processor until the nuts are finely chopped. Add the nut butter and pulse to combine. With the motor running, add the dates a few at a time. Process until all the dates are added and the mixture comes together, adding 1 teaspoon cold water if necessary. The mixture should be soft and pliable. Remove it from the food processor and bring it together completely with your hands.

3 Roll heaped teaspoons of the date mixture into balls. Roll the truffles in the chopped pistachios to lightly coat, shaking off any excess. Place in an airtight container and refrigerate.

tips You can replace the carob powder with unsweetened cocoa powder or raw cacao powder.

These truffles will keep in an airtight container in the refrigerator for up to 2 weeks. Remove them from the refrigerator 10 minutes before serving.

vegan (see tips)

Although rice pudding is traditionally made with white rice, this wholegrain brown-rice version has a delicious nutty flavour and is far higher in fibre, with anti-inflammatory properties. Strawberries are naturally low in sugar, yet packed with the antioxidant vitamin C.

Creamy coconut rice with caramelised strawberries

Preparation time: 10 minutes
Cooking time: 30 minutes
Serves 4

585 g (3 cups) cooked medium-grain brown rice

400 ml (14 fl oz) can reduced-fat coconut milk

185 ml (3/4 cup) reduced-fat milk (see tips)

2 tablespoons coconut sugar

1 cinnamon stick

CARAMELISED STRAWBERRIES

250 g (9 oz) punnet strawberries, hulled and halved

2 teaspoons coconut sugar

1 Put the cooked rice, coconut milk, milk, coconut sugar and cinnamon stick in a large saucepan over medium heat. Bring to the boil, then reduce the heat to low and simmer, stirring occasionally, for 20–25 minutes or until thick and creamy. Set aside to cool slightly (see tips).

2 When you are ready to serve, make the caramelised strawberries. Heat a large frying pan over medium–high heat and add the strawberries and 2 teaspoons of water. Sprinkle the sugar over the strawberries. Cook, stirring occasionally, for 1–2 minutes or until the strawberries are slightly caramelised.

3 To serve, divide the rice pudding among serving glasses or bowls, and top with some caramelised strawberries and any pan juices.

tips This rice pudding can be served warm or at room temperature.

The trick to making a creamy brown-rice pudding is to cook the rice first, otherwise it can take over an hour of stirring!

For a vegan version, use unsweetened soy, almond or coconut milk.

pantry basics

vegan

Home-made nut butter is easy to make and loaded with healthy fats. If it's too thick, add a little macadamia oil, to achieve the consistency you want.

Roasted nut and cacao butter

Preparation time: 10 minutes
Cooking time: 10 minutes
Makes 480 g (3 cups)

155 g (1 cup) unsalted raw cashew nuts

155 g (1 cup) unsalted natural almonds

155 g (1 cup) unsalted raw macadamia nuts

2 tablespoons raw cacao powder, sifted

1 teaspoon natural vanilla extract

1 Preheat the oven to 160°C (320°F). Line a large baking tray with baking paper. Spread the nuts in a single layer on the tray and roast for 10 minutes or until light golden. Set aside to cool (see tips).

2 Transfer the nuts to a high-powered blender or food processor. Blend on high speed for 6–8 minutes or until the nuts have formed a thick paste, scraping down the sides of the blender every 1–2 minutes. Add the cacao and vanilla and process until well combined.

tips The time it takes for the nuts to form a paste will depend on the power of your blender. Processing them while they're still slightly warm helps them break down a little more quickly.

This nut butter will keep in an airtight jar in a cool dark place for up to 1 month.

vegan

Try this nutritious spread on crackers or use it as a dip with vegetable sticks. It can even stand in as an anti-inflammatory alternative for cheese sauce (see page 168).

Cashew cheese

Preparation time: 10 minutes
(plus 3 hours soaking)
Cooking time: None
Makes 400 g (2 cups)

235 g (1½ cups) unsalted raw cashew nuts

1 tablespoon lemon juice

2 teaspoons white wine vinegar

2 teaspoons dijon mustard (see tips)

125 ml (½ cup) reduced-fat coconut milk or water (see tips)

1 Place the cashews in a large bowl, cover with cold water and soak for 3 hours. Drain.

2 Combine the cashews, lemon juice, vinegar and mustard in a blender. Blend on high speed, gradually adding the coconut milk, until the cashews are smooth and have the consistency of thick cream cheese.

tips Dijon mustard should be gluten-free, but always check the label.

Blending the nuts with coconut milk rather than water gives a creamier result.

This cashew 'cheese' will keep in an airtight container in the fridge for up to 3 days.

vegetarian (see tips)

These crackers couldn't be easier to make: they're simply seeds, water and a little parmesan. The linseeds are essential because, when mixed with water, they form a gel that binds the ingredients and holds the crackers together. And they're an excellent source of omega-3 fatty acids.

Seed and parmesan crackers

Preparation time: 10 minutes
(plus 15 minutes soaking)
Cooking time: 55 minutes
Makes 24

55 g (1/3 cup) linseeds (flaxseeds)
55 g (1/3 cup) pepitas (pumpkin seeds)
2 tablespoons sesame seeds
2 tablespoons chia seeds
1 tablespoon poppy seeds
25 g (1/4 cup) finely grated parmesan cheese (see tips)
2 teaspoons chopped thyme
1/2 teaspoon sea salt

1 Combine the seeds in a bowl with 185 ml (3/4 cup) water and leave to soak for 15 minutes. Stir in the parmesan, thyme and salt.

2 Meanwhile, preheat the oven to 150°C (300°F). Line a 25 x 38 cm (10 x 15 inch) baking tray with baking paper.

3 Wet your hands and press the seed mixture firmly onto the tray in a very thin, even layer. Press with the back of a spoon to smooth the surface. Lightly score into 24 squares.

4 Bake for 50–55 minutes or until golden and crisp (see tips). Cool completely on the tray, then break into crackers along the score marks.

tips For a vegetarian version, use parmesan made with non-animal rennet.

These crackers will continue to harden as they cool. They can be stored in an airtight container for up to 1 week.

(pictured page 226)

vegan (see tips)

Most commercially made nut bars contain a lot of sugar. Making your own means you know exactly what goes into them. Nuts are loaded with mono- and polyunsaturated fatty acids and are very satisfying, but also extremely energy dense, so portion size is the key.

Seed and nut bars

Preparation time: 15 minutes
Cooking time: 20 minutes
Makes 20

320 g (2 cups) unsalted raw nuts, such as almonds, macadamia nuts and walnuts

75 g (½ cup) sunflower seeds

75 g (½ cup) pepitas (pumpkin seeds)

2 tablespoons chia seeds

2 tablespoons sesame seeds

2 teaspoons ground cinnamon

175 g (½ cup) single origin floral honey (see tips)

2 tablespoons macadamia oil

2 teaspoons natural vanilla extract

1 Preheat the oven to 150°C (300°F). Line a 23 x 33 cm (9 x 13 inch) baking tray with baking paper.

2 Roughly chop the nuts, sunflower seeds and pepitas together in a food processor. Transfer to a large bowl and stir in the chia, sesame seeds and cinnamon.

3 Stir the honey, oil and vanilla in a small saucepan over low heat until well combined. Pour over the dry ingredients and stir well.

4 Wet your hands and press the mixture firmly onto the tray. Press with the back of a spoon to smooth the surface. Bake for 20 minutes or until deep golden brown. Cool completely on the tray, then refrigerate until chilled. Cut into bars or squares.

tips For a vegan version, replace the honey with rice malt syrup.

These will keep for up to 2 weeks in an airtight container in the fridge.

(pictured page 227)

Seed and parmesan crackers

(see recipe page 224)

Seed and nut bars

(see recipe page 225)

vegan

Chickpea flour has a wonderful nutty taste once it's cooked, and it's extremely nutritious. Like all gluten-free breads, these flatbreads are not as robust as those made with wheat flour, so handle them gently.

Currant, coconut and coriander flatbreads

Preparation time: 15 minutes (plus 1 hour resting)
Cooking time: 15 minutes
Makes 4

145 g (1 cup) chickpea flour (besan)

1 tablespoon extra virgin olive oil, plus extra for brushing

2 tablespoons coriander (cilantro) leaves, finely chopped

2 tablespoons desiccated (shredded) coconut

1½ tablespoons currants

1 Sift the chickpea flour into a large bowl. Gradually add 185 ml (¾ cup) water, whisking until well combined, then continue to whisk for 1–2 minutes or until smooth. Whisk in the olive oil. Cover and set aside to rest for 1 hour.

2 Stir in the coriander, coconut, currants and a large pinch of sea salt. Heat a non-stick frying pan over medium–high heat and brush with a little extra olive oil. Ladle in a quarter of the batter (about 60 ml/¼ cup) and tilt the pan to spread the batter out to a 15 cm (6 inch) diameter circle.

3 Cook for 2 minutes or until bubbles start to appear on the surface. Carefully flip, and cook for a further 1–2 minutes or until golden and cooked through. Transfer to a plate and keep warm. Repeat with the remaining batter to make 4 flatbreads.

tip These flatbreads are best eaten straight away.

Cauliflower is low in kilojoules, packed with fibre and a great source of vitamin C, with just one cup containing 50% of your RDI. It makes a great low-carb alternative to regular rice or couscous and can be flavoured with just about anything. Here are three of my favourite flavour combos.

Cauliflower rice, three ways

Preparation time: 10 minutes
Cooking time: 10 minutes
Serves 4

1 small head (700 g/1 lb 9 oz) cauliflower, broken into florets

2 teaspoons macadamia oil

1 onion, finely chopped

2 teaspoons brown mustard seeds

2 garlic cloves, crushed

1 long fresh green chilli, finely chopped

¼ cup fresh curry leaves

1 Process the cauliflower in a food processor, in batches, until it resembles rice.

2 Heat the oil in a large wok over high heat. Add the onion and stir-fry for 2 minutes. Add the mustard seeds, garlic, chilli and curry leaves and stir-fry for 1 minute or until fragrant. Add the cauliflower and stir-fry for 2–3 minutes or until just tender. Season with salt and freshly ground black pepper. Serve.

Chilli, ginger and coriander

In step 2, heat 2 teaspoons macadamia oil in the wok. Add 1 chopped long red chilli, 2 teaspoons grated ginger and 1 crushed garlic clove and stir-fry for 1 minute or until fragrant. Add the cauliflower and stir-fry for 2–3 minutes or until just tender. Stir in 3 tablespoons chopped coriander (cilantro) and season to taste.

Cumin, currant and parsley

In step 2, heat 2 teaspoons extra virgin olive oil in the wok and stir-fry 1 chopped red onion for 2 minutes. Add 2 teaspoons ground cumin and 2 teaspoons grated lemon zest and stir-fry for 1 minute or until fragrant. Add the cauliflower and stir-fry for 2–3 minutes or until just tender. Stir in 1 tablespoon currants and 2 tablespooons chopped parsley and season well.

vegetarian • dairy free

Milled from sorghum grain, sorghum flour has a light, sweet and nutty flavour and is not as grainy as rice flour, so ideal to use in baking. The sorghum flour mix is a fantastic basic flour blend to use in recipes such as pizza bases or bread. Likewise, the sorghum and almond flour mix is ideal to use in muffins and cakes.

Sorghum flour blend

Makes 4 cups

280 g (2 cups) white sorghum flour (see tip) or 320 g (2 cups) white rice flour

260 g (1½ cups) potato starch

65 g (½ cup) tapioca flour (starch)

1½ teaspoons xanthan gum

Sift together all ingredients and keep in an airtight jar.

tip For a wholemeal version, use 320 g (2 cups) brown rice flour instead of sorghum flour.

Sorghum and almond flour blend

Makes 2½ cups

140 g (1 cup) sorghum flour

175 g (1 cup) potato starch

50 g (½ cup) almond meal

¾ teaspoon xanthan gum

Sift together all ingredients and keep in an airtight jar.

Pizza base

Preparation time: 25 minutes
Cooking time: 20–25 minutes
Makes 4 x 22 cm (8½ inch) pizzas

180 ml (¾ cup) tepid water

7 g (¼ oz) dried yeast

2 teaspoons single origin floral honey

400 g (2½ cups) sorghum flour blend (see left)

1 teaspoon sea salt

60 ml (¼ cup) extra virgin olive oil, plus extra to drizzle

2 egg whites, lightly beaten

1 Preheat the oven to 220°C (425°F). Line 2 large round baking trays with baking paper. Whisk together the water, yeast and honey in a jug. Set aside in a warm place until frothy, about 10 minutes.

2 Sift the sorghum flour blend and salt into a large bowl. Make a well in the centre, add the oil, egg whites and yeast mixture and stir with a wooden spoon to form a soft dough. Bring together with your hands and knead for 30 seconds, or until smooth.

3 Divide the dough into four. Spread or roll 2 pieces of dough on the trays, forming 2 thin, 22 cm (8½ inch) rounds. Cover with a damp cloth and leave in a warm place for 20 minutes or slightly risen.

4 Top with your favourite pizza toppings, drizzle with a little oil and bake for 10–12 minutes, until the base is crisp. Repeat with the remaining dough.

tip Add 3 tablespoons grated parmesan cheese or 2 tablespoons finely chopped herbs to the dough.

vegan (see tips)

The addition of buckwheat flour, almond meal and chia seeds make this gluten-free bread high in protein, fibre and essential fatty acids. Almonds are also rich in vitamin E, a powerful antioxidant known to reduce inflammation.

Almond, chia and seed bread

Preparation time: 10 minutes
Cooking time: 50–55 minutes
Makes 12 slices

- **140 g (1 cup) buckwheat flour**
- **65 g (1/2 cup) tapioca flour**
- **1 1/2 teaspoons bicarbonate of soda (baking soda)**
- **100 g (1 cup) almond meal**
- **40 g (1/4 cup) sunflower seeds, plus 2 teaspoons extra**
- **45 g (1/4 cup) pepitas (pumpkin seeds), plus 2 teaspoons extra**
- **50 g (1/3 cup) chia seeds**
- **large pinch of salt**
- **1 teaspoon single origin floral honey (see tips)**
- **1 tablespoon apple cider vinegar**
- **Extra virgin olive oil spray**

1 Sift the buckwheat flour, tapioca flour and bicarbonate of soda into a large bowl. Stir in the almond meal, sunflower seeds, pepitas, chia seeds and salt. Make a well in the centre.

2 Combine the honey, vinegar and 450 ml (1 3/4 cups) water in a jug. Add the wet ingredients to the dry ingredients and stir until well combined; the mixture will be very wet. Cover and place in a warm place for 1 hour to rest. Mixture will thicken as it stands.

3 Preheat the oven to 180°C (350°F). Lightly spray a 10 x 20 cm (4 x 8 inch) non-stick loaf tin with oil. Line the base and long sides with baking paper, extending over the sides. Spoon the dough into the prepared tin. Sprinkle the top with extra seeds. Bake for 50–55 minutes or until a skewer inserted into the centre comes out clean. Set aside to cool in the tin for 10 minutes before carefully transferring to a wire rack to cool completely. Cut into slices to serve.

tips This bread freezes well. Cut it into slices and wrap individually in plastic wrap and freeze for up to 1 month.

Substitute the honey with rice malt syrup for a vegan version.

dairy free

Golden mylk is a delicious alternative to coffee without the caffeine. The active compound in turmeric, curcumin, acts as a powerful antioxidant with many associated health benefits, including being a natural anti-inflammatory.

Golden mylk

Preparation time: 10 minutes
Cooking time: 15 minutes
Serves 1

2 teaspoons golden paste (see below)

250 ml (1 cup) unsweetened almond, coconut or soy milk

1–2 teaspoons single origin floral honey

½ teaspoon vanilla extract

Ground cinnamon, to serve

GOLDEN PASTE

100 g (3¾ oz) fresh turmeric, peeled (see tips)

30 g (¼ cup) grated fresh ginger

1 tablespoon extra virgin coconut oil

2 teaspoons ground cinnamon

1 teaspoon ground cardamom

½–1 teaspoon ground black pepper

1 To make the golden paste, finely grate the turmeric. Blend the turmeric, ginger and 185 ml (¾ cup) water in a blender until smooth. Transfer to a medium saucepan and place over low heat. Cook, stirring, for 8–10 minutes or until thick. Remove from heat, whisk in the coconut oil and spices and transfer to a sterilised jar (see tips).

2 To make golden mylk, place 2 teaspoons of the golden paste in a small saucepan with your milk of choice, honey and vanilla. Heat over low heat until it reaches your desired temperature. Serve sprinkled with a little extra cinnamon.

tips Wear gloves when peeling turmeric to prevent it from staining your hands.

Golden paste will keep in a sealed sterilised jar in the fridge for up to 2 weeks.

dairy free

Green tea is rich in polyphenols, plant compounds that act as potent antioxidants and play an important role in protecting the body against chronic inflammation. I like to make a big jug of green tea and keep it chilled in the fridge, to drink throughout the day.

Iced green tea, three ways

Lemongrass, ginger and mint

Preparation time: 5 minutes
Cooking time: 10 minutes
Makes 6 cups

3 cm (1¼ inch) piece ginger, peeled, thinly sliced

1 lemongrass stem, cut into 4 cm (1½ inch) lengths, bruised

2–3 green tea bags

½ cup fresh mint leaves

1 Combine the ginger, lemongrass and 1.5 litres (6 cups) water in a large saucepan and bring to the boil. Add the tea bags and half the mint leaves, remove from the heat and set aside to steep, covered, for 5 minutes.

2 Strain the tea, discarding the solids. Refrigerate the tea until chilled. Add the remaining mint to serve.

Honey and lemon

Combine the juice and zest of 1 lemon with 1.5 litres (6 cups) water in a large saucepan and bring to the boil. Add 2–3 green tea bags and 2 tablespoons single origin floral honey, remove from the heat and leave to steep, covered, for 5 minutes. Strain, discarding the solids, and refrigerate to chill. Add 1 sliced lemon to serve.

Raspberry and lime

In a large saucepan bring 1.5 litres (6 cups) water to the boil. Add 2–3 green tea bags and 1 tablespoon single origin floral honey, the juice of 1 lime and 125 g (1 cup) fresh or frozen raspberries. Remove from the heat and set aside to steep, covered, for 5 minutes. Strain, discarding the solids, and refrigerate to chill. Add 1 sliced lime to serve.

two-week anti-inflammatory meal planner

WEEK ONE

MONDAY

Breakfast: Quinoa and cranberry porridge with power seed sprinkle, *page 15*

Snack: Roasted sweet potato and cashew hummus, *page 34*

Lunch: Brown rice salad with peanuts, *page 70*

Snack: 1 handful of walnuts plus ½ cup of blueberries

Dinner: Chia-crusted salmon with Asian greens and soy dressing, *page 134*

TUESDAY

Breakfast: Nutty buckwheat granola with dates and seeds, *page 14*

Snack: 2 wholegrain rice cakes topped with avocado

Lunch: Moroccan chicken soup, *page 93*

Snack: Golden mylk, *page 232*

Dinner: Tofu and vegetable curry with raita, *page 94*

WEDNESDAY

Breakfast: Sweet potato toast with poached egg, avocado, tomato and herb salad, *page 19*

Snack: Honey spice roasted chickpeas, *page 35*

Lunch: Kale, quinoa and mint tabouleh, *page 75*

Snack: 20 g tamari almonds plus 1 kiwifruit

Dinner: Beef and veggie lasagna, *page 162*

THURSDAY

Breakfast: Muesli with dried apple, pepitas and almonds, *page 12*

Snack: ½ cup of veggie sticks with 2 tablespoons of hummus

Lunch: Pumpkin, bean and coconut soup, *page 80*

Snack: Seed and nut bars, *page 225*, plus ½ cup of raspberries

Dinner: Fish tacos with spiced tomato and toasted coconut salad, *page 124*

FRIDAY

Breakfast: Berry smoothie with avocado and coconut water, *page 20*

Snack: Kale chips, *page 43*

Lunch: Roasted broccoli and chickpea salad with herbed tahini dressing, *page 58*

Snack: 150 g natural yoghurt topped with berries and chopped walnuts

Dinner: Spiced chicken tray bake, *page 118*

SATURDAY

Breakfast: Almond, chia and seed bread spread with ¼ avocado, *page 231*

Snack: Honey spice roasted chickpeas, *page 35*

Lunch: Salmon, quinoa and dill fish cakes, *page 137*

Snack: 1 cup of soy milk blended with 2 teaspoons chia seeds and ½ cup of any frozen fruit

Dinner: Turkey larb in cos lettuce cups, *page 102*

SUNDAY

Breakfast: Baked eggs and beans with hummus toasts, *page 27*

Snack: Golden mylk, *page 232*

Lunch: Bruschetta with broad beans and marinated capsicums, *page 46*

Snack: Peanut butter cups, *page 213*, plus 1 cup of grapes

Dinner: Cauliflower crust pizza with white beans, pumpkin and cherry tomatoes, *page 175*

WEEK TWO

MONDAY

Breakfast: Green zing smoothie with mango and chia, *page 20*

Snack: Seed and nut bars, *page 225*

Lunch: Rice salad with roasted pumpkin, beans and orange spice dressing, *page 64*

Snack: ½ cup of veggie sticks with 2 tablespoons of hummus

Dinner: Macadamia-crusted fish with garlic greens, *page 128*

TUESDAY

Breakfast: Almond, chia and seed bread topped with 2 teaspoons of nut butter and 6 sliced strawberries, *page 231*

Snack: 1 cup of soy milk blended with 2 teaspoons chia seeds and ½ cup frozen fruit

Lunch: Raw beetroot and lentil salad with mustard dressing, *page 62*

Snack: Vanilla almond cakes, *page 206*

Dinner: Baked turkey meatballs, *page 112*

WEDNESDAY

Breakfast: Nutty buckwheat granola with dates and seeds, *page 14*

Snack: Quinoa, feta, roasted capsicum and corn muffins, *page 52*

Lunch: Poached chicken, broad bean and apple salad with toasted seeds, *page 110*

Snack: 1 handful of macadamia nuts plus 1 mandarin

Dinner: Lentil and quinoa pilaf with roasted vegetables, *page 184*

THURSDAY

Breakfast: 150 g natural yoghurt topped with berries and walnuts

Snack: 1 handful of pepitas plus 2 fresh dates

Lunch: Falafel with tomato and radish salad, *page 49*

Snack: Cannellini bean, tuna and caper dip, *page 32*

Dinner: Ginger beef and bean stir-fry, *page 146*

FRIDAY

Breakfast: Kale eggs with smoked salmon and broccolini, *page 18*

Snack: 1 handful of almonds plus 1 cup berries

Lunch: Chickpea, tomato and quinoa soup with pesto toasts, *page 82*

Snack: Golden mylk, *page 232*

Dinner: Barbecued trout parcels with fennel, zucchini and tomato, *page 136*

SATURDAY

Breakfast: Choc chia, coconut and blueberry pots, *page 23*

Snack: 2 wholegrain rice cakes spread with tahini and topped with sliced tomato

Lunch: Rice salad with roasted pumpkin, beans and orange spice dressing, *page 64*

Snack: Edamame with chilli salt, *page 42*

Dinner: Pork satays with pickled carrot salad, *page 164*

SUNDAY

Breakfast: Butter bean, chilli and corn fritters with cucumber salad, *page 26*

Snack: Banana bread, *page 22*

Lunch: Buckwheat and grilled chicken summer salad, *page 56*

Snack: 1 handful of tamari almonds, plus ½ cup of berries

Dinner: Baked sweet potatoes stuffed with spinach, feta and pepitas, *page 171*

index

d

e

f

g

h

j

k

t

v

z

Published in 2019 by Murdoch Books, an imprint of Allen & Unwin
Some of the recipes in this book were previously published in *Supergrains* (2013), *Superlegumes* (2015) and *Real Delicious* (2016), all by Chrissy Freer.
Reprinted 2020(x3)

Murdoch Books Australia
83 Alexander Street,
Crows Nest, NSW 2065
Phone: +61 (0)2 8425 0100
murdochbooks.com.au
info@murdochbooks.com.au

Murdoch Books UK
Ormond House, 26–27 Boswell Street,
London, WC1N 3JZ
Phone: +44 (0) 20 8785 5995
murdochbooks.co.uk
info@murdochbooks.co.uk

For Corporate Orders & Custom Publishing contact our business development team at salesenquiries@murdochbooks.com.au

Publisher: Corinne Roberts
Editorial Manager: Jane Price
Designer: Susanne Geppert
Editor: Shan Wolody
Photographer: Julie Renouf
Production Director: Lou Playfair

ISBN 978 1 76052 531 6 Australia

A cataloguing-in-publication entry is available from the catalogue of the National Library of Australia at nla.gov.au

Printed in China by C&C Offset Printing Co. Ltd.

Disclaimer: The content presented in this book is meant for inspiration and informational purposes only. The purchaser of this book understands that the author is not a medical professional, and the information contained within this book is not intended to replace medical advice or meant to be relied upon to treat, cure, or prevent any disease, illness, or medical condition. It is understood that you will seek full medical clearance by a licensed physician before making any changes mentioned in this book. The author and publisher claim no responsibility to any person or entity for any liability, loss, or damage caused or alleged to be caused directly or indirectly as a result of the use, application, or interpretation of the material in this book.

The paper in this book is FSC® certified. FSC® promotes environmentally responsible, socially beneficial and economically viable management of the world's forests.